I0002916

Foreword

Dear Reader,

for system-malfunctions there is only one way: Selected step-by-step guidance and professional repair functions that you can recover your system. Because if Windows 8 fails to respond, you will no longer have access to your e-mail and the Internet - this means stress, especially if you are work-related dependent on your PC.

Reiner Backer

Author of Windows 8 Troubleshooting

The helpful diagnostic and repair guidance to make Windows 8 work again, in an emergency, you will find in this book. So you are immediately capable to repair your system and recover important data, in the case of an error – even from a dead hard drive.

Did you know, for an example, that there are free scripts from Microsoft that help you to fix system breakdowns 8 Windows automatically?

Whether you want to eliminate an error message, change configuration settings, or solve other problems, **Microsoft Fix it** offers many solutions that can be easily accomplished automatically, without the need for manual intervention.

1   Search with Google (www.google.de) and the search request **Microsoft Fix it** for the Microsoft help.

2   Click the **Microsoft Fix it Solution Center** link.

3   In the upper section, select the ❶ product, which poses a problem.

4   Below you will get a ❷ list of solutions. Select the suitable solution with one click on **Run Now**.

5   You will then usually be offered a .MSI file to download to solve the problem. This file can be saved first directly or can be started by running the file after the download.

6   Follow the instructions in the assistant.

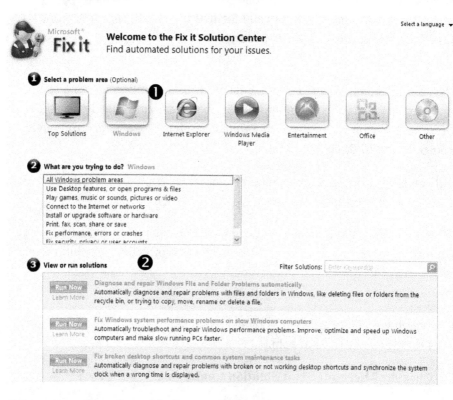

Solve system disorders with the repair-script by Microsoft.

Table of Contents

Table of Contents

Table of Contents

Table of Contents

Table of Contents

Standard tools of Windows 8

If your system will not boot or is crashing regularly, the in-built Windows system functions are often the last rescue. In safe mode a start is usually still possible. You can then reset your system, for example, with the system restore to a stable state.

Back up your complete system

Who himself had once been struggling with a dead hard drive knows how much work it is to reinstall the operating system and all programs. A lot less time-consuming is, create disk images of your system regularly. After a hard drive crash, it is then sufficient to install a new hard drive, play back the image and everything works as before.

So you are, in case of damage, able to transfer back all of the previously saved, in the image file, data, programs and operating system. This works even if Windows is damaged or if your hard drive has completely failed to respond.

To create an image of your hard disk

In Windows 8, a backup imaging tool is included. In an emergency, you can then set up your system and all your files and programs easily with the image restore. For a complex system, with 200 GB of unused space, that can take even about three hours. But the re-uploading of your applications and data is fully automatic, without you having to do anything.

Tip! Save the image on an external USB hard drive. So you are in the event of a hard drive failure secured and can restore the system. Alternatively, you can also create multiple DVDs or use an USB stick.

Standard tools of Windows 8

1 Press the key combination **<WIN> + X** and select the entry  **Control Panel**. If you are on the desktop, you can also click the start button with the rake mouse button.

Task Manager
Control Panel ❶
File Explorer

Select the stripped down start menu of Windows 8.

2 Choose from **View by** the entry ❷ **Large icons**.

3 Click ❸ **Windows 7 File Recovery**.

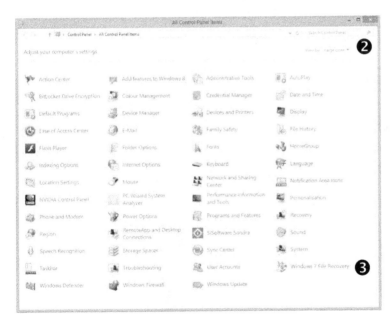

You can view the functions in the Control Panel individually.

9

4   In the left part of the window **❹** choose **Create a system image**.

5   Below you can choose whether you are on a **❺** hard drive and want to save on DVDs or on a network share, the image of the hard drive.

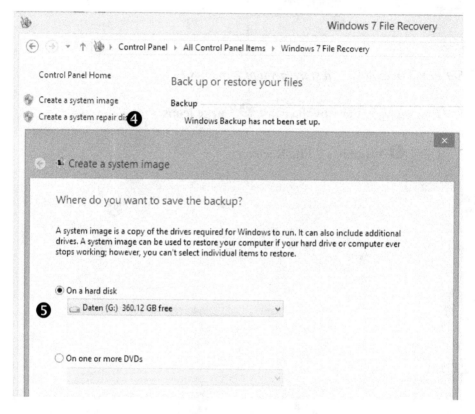

Create an exact copy of your hard drive.

6   Confirm your choice by clicking on **Next** and choose what to back up drives.

7   Then click **Next** and ❻ **Start backup**.

Start the backup process.

8   Let us finally with a click on **Yes** create a bootable CD. About this CD, you can back up your system and the failure of your hard drive.

Set Windows back to the last working state

Who does not know, at some point, due installation or a crash of Windows it comes to error messages or becomes unstable. Now, it would help to cancel the last action before the occurrence of the error. But the error caused is not always this clear.

For such cases, Windows 8 provides System Restore. So that you can reset your system in disturbances or other problems quickly, to get back in the condition it was, before the problem occurred. Windows 8 operating system uses previously, for this purpose, saved settings, including device drivers and files.

- Each time you update your system or a hardware device driver, Windows 8 automatically creates a restore point. Requirement is that enough disk space i on the hard disk available and the System Restore is not disabled.

- A restore point is created also includes the installation of software components when they perform changes to the system files or settings. This is an example for an update or security patch from Windows 8 the case.

Set a restore point

In case of an error you can undo the changes on your system, which have been made before, with the System Restore. The saved configuration is restored and everything is back the way it was before the change. Therefore you should manually set up the a restore point at first. Proceed as follows:

1   Navigate by clicking on the ❶ **Desktop tile** on the Windows desktop.

Standard tools of Windows 8

*On the Home page, click the **Desktop tile**.*

2   Press the key combination <**WIN**> + <**X**> or click the start button with the rake mouse button.

3   Select the Entry ❷ **Control Panel**.

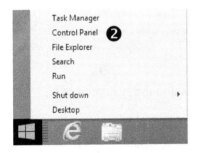

Activate the Control Panel.

4   Choose from **View by** the entry ❸ **Large icons**.

5   Click ❹ **System** in the left part of the window and on the link ❺ **System protection**.

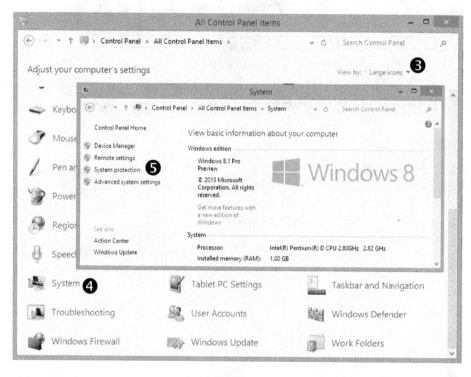

*Select the link **System protection**.*

6   Here you can select the volumes to be included in the system restore. Leave it best at the default setting.

7   Should the protection for the drive in question be disabled, click **Configure** and select the option to **Turn on system protection**.

8   To create a restore point, click now on **❻ Create**.

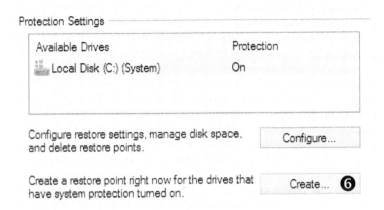

Prepare for emergencies a manual restore point.

9   Enter a ❼ name for the restore point a.

10 Click on **Create**. The restore point will be created and thus a snapshot of your system stored.

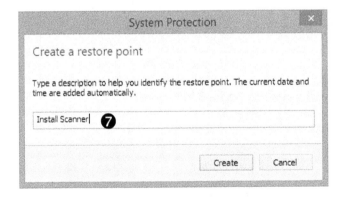

Assign a meaningful name.

When a problem or damage in case, you can now roll back your system to a previous, working state.

1   Activate the **Control Panel** (**<WIN>+<X>**) and choose **Large icons**.

2   Click on **System** and in the left part of the window on the link **System protection**.

3   Click on ❽ **System Restore** and **Next**.

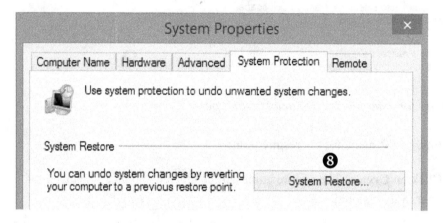

Enable the system restore.

4   Select the ❾ restore point click the ❿ **Next** button.

5   Confirm your selection by clicking on **Finish**.

6   Your system is then restarted and restored to the previously selected working state.

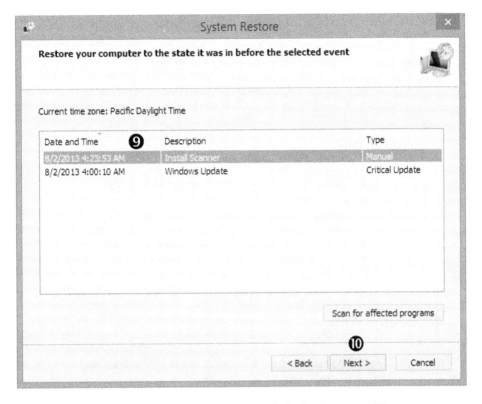

To reset your system with just a few mouse clicks back to a stable state.

Select Safe Mode

If Windows suddenly freezes at the startup or breaks down with a blue screen, safe mode is often the last resort. Because after starting in safe mode, make the necessary corrections in the Windows settings and get your system back up and running again. In Safe Mode, your system starts up only with the drivers, services and processes that are essential for a minimum operation of Windows.

This includes the drivers for the mouse, monitor, keyboard, hard disk, the basic settings for the graphics engine and the standard system services. Especially after the failed installation of new equipment, or software drivers Windows automatically starts in safe mode.

Set the Safe Mode with these problems:

- Windows does not respond to input or "freezes".

- Errors occurs during the work, such as a "STOP"-error.

- After a configuration change or new hardware is installed, the system will not boot.

- The screen output is wrong.

To boot your system into safe mode

Safe mode you can enable Windows 8 as following:

1   To start Windows 8 targeted in safe mode, press while your system start the keys **<Shift>+<F8>**. The boot time of Windows 8 is very fast and therefore this step often works after a few tries.

2   Windows 8 should still start, you can also activate the system using the System Configuration.

3   To do this, press the key combination **<WIN>+<R>**. Enter ❶ **msconfig** and press the **OK** button.

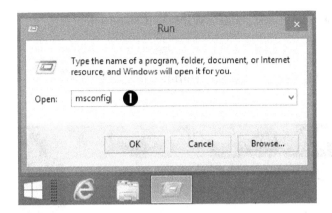

Activate the command prompt.

4   In the tab **Boot**, enable the option ❷ **Safe boot** and start the system new.

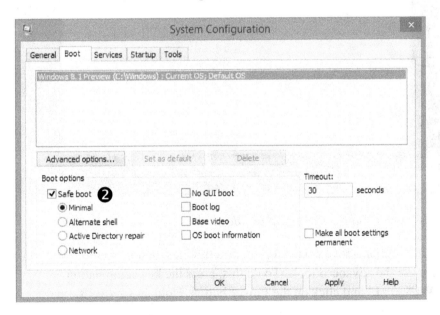

Start the System Configuration in safe mode.

5 Press the key combination in safe mode **<WIN>+<X>** and select the **Control Panel** item.

6 Enter in the search field, type the text ❸ **trouble** and select the ❹ appropriate link from.

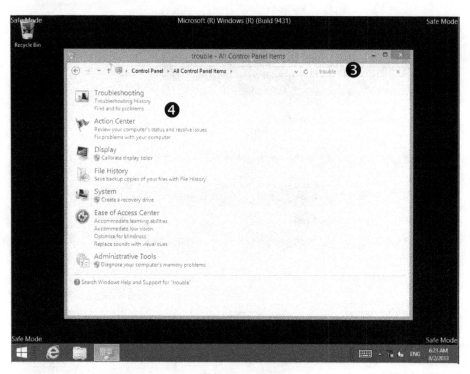

All features of Windows 8 are also in safe mode.

7 If the solution above does not provide a troubleshooting solution, you can also use the advanced tools. To do this, press the key combination **<WIN>+<I>** and click on the **Power** button. Hold down **<Shift>** and click **Restart**.

8   Then click on ❺ **Troubleshoot** and for example **Refresh your PC**. Then the system is scanned for errors and automatically repair them.

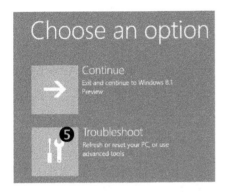

Insert the rescue capabilities of Windows 8.

9   If the problem does not solve, click **Advanced options**.

10   Choose for example the ❻ **Startup Repair** to fix problems that prevent Windows from loading.

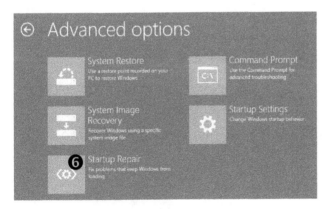

Recover Windows 8 on a few clicks.

Note: To start at boot comfortably in safe mode, there is a trick. With this, you can enable the boot menu as the previous versions of Windows used with **<F8>**:

1   Press the key combination **<WIN>+<X>**.

2   Select from the menu the entry ❼ **Windows PowerShell (Admin)**.

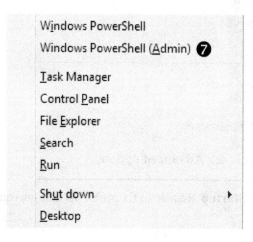

Activate the command prompt with elevated privileges.

3   Confirm the User Account Control by clicking **Yes**.

4   Enter the two following ❽ commands:
cd \ <Return>
bcdedit / set {default} bootmenupolicy legacy <Return>

5   Close the command prompt. Afterwards the start menu of the safe mode, can be activated via **<F8>** on startup again.

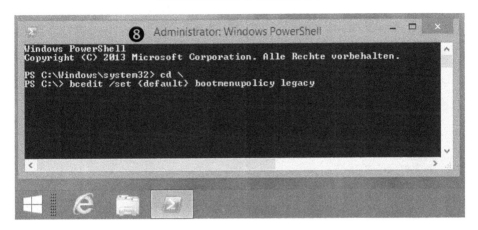

To enable the safe mode as usual.

Check your hard disk for errors

In indefinable and surprising disk problems, you should first access to software tools. Windows offers for this case, the disk check. To enable this, follow these steps:

1   Close all programs and files and start the Windows Explorer
(**<WIN>+<E>**.

2   In Windows Explorer, right-click the drive you want to check for error.
From the context menu select the ❶ **Properties** entry.

Enable the Check Disk from Windows Explorer.

3   Select the ❷ **Tools** tab and click ❸ **Check**.

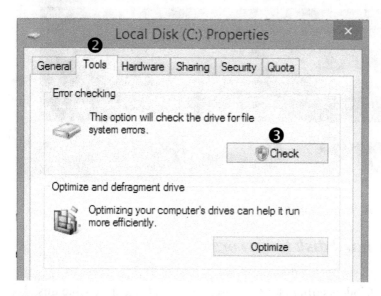

Start the disk check.

4 Click the link ❹ **Scan drive**.

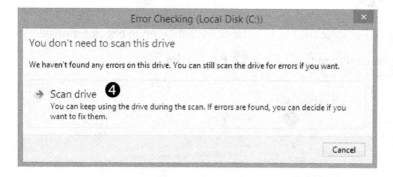

Check your file system for errors and let it repair automatically.

4   During 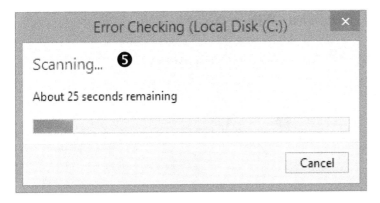 during the check of the drive, you can continue working. If errors are discovered in the file system, you can have them repaired automatically.

Depending on the size of the hard drive test can take about 5 minutes.

Tip! Should now still be displayed errors in the file system, run the **chkdsk** command. This command-line tool offers extensive possibilities for inspecting a hard drive.

1   Press **<WIN>+<X>** and select the entry **Windows PowerShell (Admin)**.

2   Enter the **chkdsk** command with the drive letter: **chkdsk c:** and press **<Return>**. If you do not specify the drive letter, the default is C: drive under investigation.

Repair the system files of Windows 8

If important system files of Windows 8 are damaged, nothing will work. At startup, error messages appear, important programs no longer start. Debt are defect system files, which were damaged, for example by other programs or tools. The good news: you can recover the system files very quickly.

To set the system restore files

The system files you can restore Windows 8 only with administrator privileges in the command prompt. To do this follow the following step-by-step guide:

1   Press the key combination **<WIN>+<X>**.

2   Select the entry ❶ **Windows PowerShell (Admin)**.

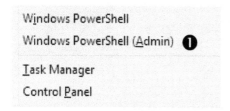

Activate the command prompt with elevated privileges.

3   Enter ❷ **sfc /scannnow** and confirm with **<Return>**.

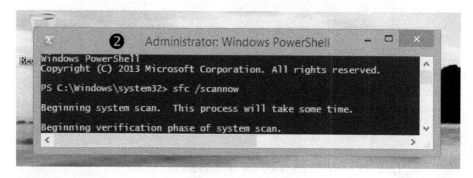

Start checking of system files.

Solve network problems

For most problems associated with network connections you should first start in the Windows 8 built-in network diagnostic utility to identify the cause of the problem.

To eliminate connection problems with Network Diagnostics

In order to eliminate interference in the network, follow the following step-by-step guide:

1   Press the key combination <**WIN**>+<**X**> and select the **Control Panel** item.

2   Choose from **View by** the entry **Category**.

3   Click **System and Security – Action Center**.

4   Select the link ❶ **Troubleshooting**.

Let problems automatically be detected and fixed.

27

5 On the next window, under **Network and Internet**, click the link ❷ **Connect to the internet**.

With the network diagnostics, see the error quickly.

6 On the next window, click ❸ Next. Now the Network Diagnostics gathers configuration information, and if possible to provide automatic recovery for the network connection by.

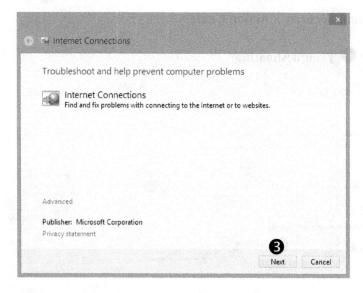

Follow the wizard to solve the problem.

Test different boot options

If you get a clear error message at startup, you know the cause of the problem. If the start in the safe mode is not possible, you can usually easily fix the system failure. Often, it's enough to update the driver.

However, sometimes the system freezes at startup and you will not get any clues about the cause. Then you need to first find out, what caused the error. To do this, use various custom boots with the System Configuration program.

Insert the System Configuration program

To run different custom system startup:

1   Press the key combination **<WIN>+<R>**.

2   Type **msconfig** and press **<Return>**.

3   Klick on ❶ **General** tab and select the ❷ **Selective startup** option.

4   Select what has to be ❸ executed at system startup.

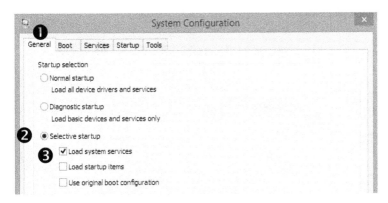

Determine what is to be run at system startup.

29

5   If the error is thrown in the subsequent steps, you know where to look. If
     the fault occurs, for example, by disabling the option ❸ **Load startup
     items** (see previous page) to, click on the **Startup** tab and on the link
     Open Task Manager.

6   Click on the **Startup** tab and uncheck the series after the ❹ Programs
     until the error no longer occurs.

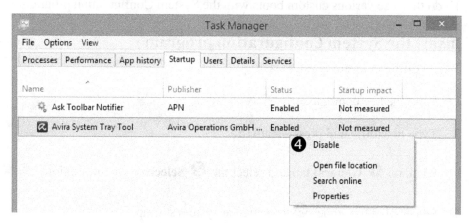

Turn on Windows 8, the startup programs in Task Manager.

7   When you have eliminated the error, re-enable the option ❺ **Normal
     Startup**.

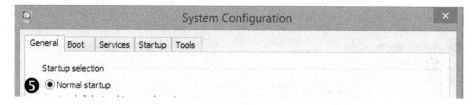

Let's start Windows normally.

30

Tip! Programs that Windows loads automatically at startup, but which will not be used by you, are unnecessary and slow down the boot time considerably. Look at the list closer to uncheck the unnecessary programs. Then your system will start faster.

Back up the system password and reset a forgotten password back

No one is safe, suddenly forgetting an important password. Therefore create a password reset medium. Windows 8 has this useful feature that allows you to recover a forgotten password.

To back up the system password and put it in an emergency restore

Windows 8 includes a convenient feature that allows you to store your password and restore in case of emergency:

1   To secure the system password, press <**WIN**>+<**X**> and select the item **Control Panel**.

2   At the top right of the search field type ❶ **password**.

3   Click on the User Accounts on the ❷ **Create a password reset disk** link.

4   Follow the ❸ instructions in the wizard.

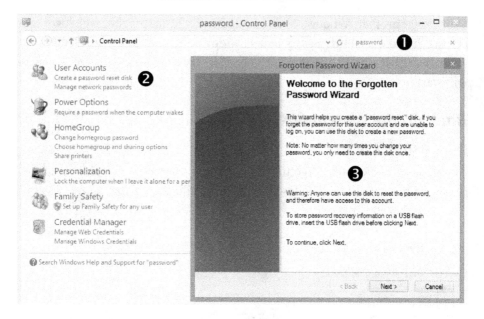

Save the system password on an external drive.

Note: You do not need a backup disk, the backup will be on any media you want.

In an emergency, you set the system password as follows: If you enter an incorrect password at login, you'll get a notice displayed. Confirm this by clicking **OK**. Then click **Reset password**, and insert the password reset disk. Does the rest of the wizard again and it will help you to create a new password.

Tip! How safe is your password, depends mostly on its length. If you are using a too short or too simple password, you will make it easy for unnecessary attackers to get at your data. Most of the users don't refer to this. Not refer to the most users. Below you will find the top ten in Germany passwords.

Standard tools of Windows 8

- Course # 1: Simple combinations of numbers, such as 12345.

- ranked No. 2: Number combinations, reminiscent of a product.

- ranked No. 3: The word password itself

- Place No. 4: pet names like honey.

- ranked No. 5: The word baby.

- ranked No. 6 seasons like summer and winter.

- ranked No. 7: The word Hello.

- ranked No. 8: Names of cities, such as Berlin, Frankfurt and Munich.

- Place No. 9: The own name.

- Place No. 10: The first name of the wife / girlfriend.

The password length should be at least 8 signs, even better would be 12. You should avoid all the words to make so-called lexical attacks. These attacks try all of the entries, of a dictionary, until the right one is finally found.

The easiest way for you to remember long passwords, in which you build this from the first letters or words of a song set.

Analyze and eliminate system problems with Event Viewer Information

If Windows takes a long time until it is fully started, it may have different reasons. In any case, you should check, if there are any problems during startup.

Set the Event Viewer to troubleshoot

With the event viewer there is also a practical diagnostic tool, which you can activate with Windows 8 as follows:

1   Press the key combination **<WIN>+<X>** and select the entry **Control System**.

2   Select **System and Security – Administrative Tools** and double-click the entry ❶ **Event Viewer**.

Tip! Alternatively you can start the Event Viewer by the key combination **<WIN>+<R>** and entering **eventvwr.msc <Return>**.

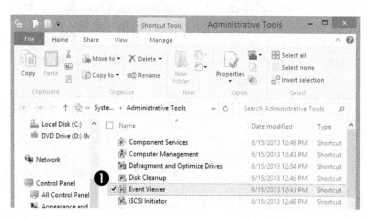

Check the log of Windows.

Select in the left pane under **Windows Logs,** which ❷ events should be displayed. In the Windows logs events from applications and events that affect the entire system or the security stored. In the Windows-logs events from applications and events, which affect the entire system or security of the system, get saved.

- **Application**: The application log records all events that are caused by programs and tools. To a database program here might be recorded a file error, for example.

- **Security**: The Security Log records security-related events. These include successful or failed logins.

- **Installation**: Find all of the events that are induced when setting up hardware and software.

- **System**: The system log can find events that have been logged by the Windows system components. Here error loadings of a device driver or startup errors get recorded, for example.

3 To get more detailed information about a record, double click on the right part of the window on the ❸ concerning event.

4 Afterwards there will be more accurate ❹ information displayed, in a separate window, about the current event.

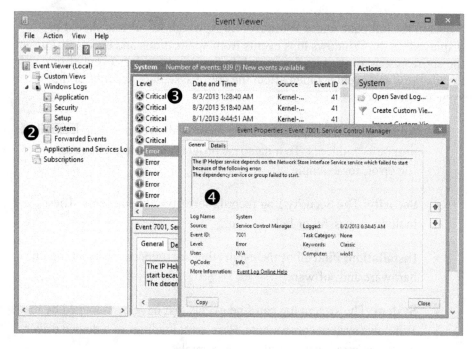

The event viewer of Windows 8.

5   In the right pane, click the column ❺ **Level**. Here, the following event types can be distinguished:

- **Error**: An error is logged if a significant problem. This is for example the case when a service at system startup can not be loaded, the program does not start or stops unexpectedly.

- **Warning**: A warning indicates a potentially insignificant event, but which indicates a potential problem. A warning is logged, for example, when there is little free disk space left.

36

- **Information**: An Information accompanies an event such as starting, stopping, or the successful execution of an application, driver, or service.

Tip! You can sort the events also. For example, click on the **Level** to display all of errors at the top of the list. When you click on ➏ **Source**, the events will be listed in order of the cause.

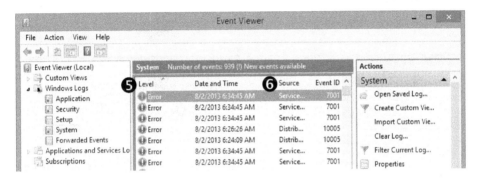

Sort the displayed events.

How to get the event properties to the error on the track

To get more information about a message, double-click in the right window of the event in question. You with the event properties are then displayed.

The following table lists, the most common event properties.

- **Error message**: Here your ➊ error message is displayed. For a first analysis, you should copy the error message you have received or a meaningful part of it, and then search in a search engine, such as www.google.de.

- **Source**: The ❷ Software that logged the event. It may be the name of an application, or a component of the system or a driver.

- **Event ID**: ❸ A number that indicates the respective event type.

- **Level**: A classification based on the importance of the event: ❹ Error, Warning, and Information.

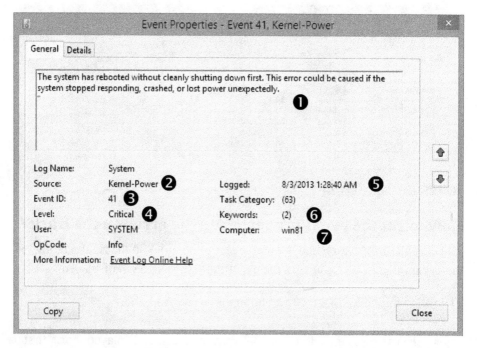

Notice the Information from the Event Properties.

- **Logs**: The local ❺ date and time of when the event occurred.

- **Keywords**: A number of ❻ categories or tags that you can use to filter or search by events.

- **Computers**: The ❼ name of the PC on which the event occurred.

Use the event ID as the key to troubleshooting

Were you unable to identify the error through Internet searches, try to analyze the malfunction of the system event ID. For each entry there is an event ID (*see point 3*).

1 You can search this Knowledge Base for Event ID in Microsoft. Enter the text ❽ **event ID** with the associated number in the search field and click the Search button.

Search among www.microsoft.com information displayed by event ID.

2   Alternatively, use the information provided by the Altair website www.eventid.net.

3   Fill in the event ID in the ❾ **Event ID** field and click on **Search**.

4   If you are still looking for the source in addition to the Event ID, enter the error under **Event Source**, as it was called in the log.

5   The database will then be searched and all reported identified results will be shown.

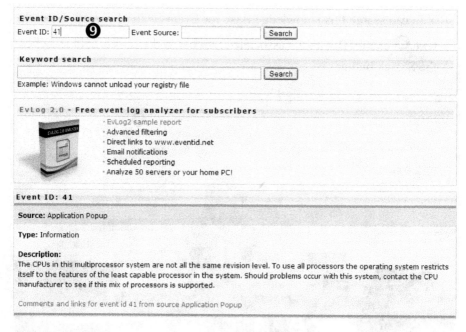

Here you will find much information about the Event ID.

Do more protection by current security patches

Periodically, Microsoft releases new drivers, system enhancements, bug fixes and security patches that you can automatically install the Windows update. These updates are important. Install them to always keep your windows up to date and to close security gaps.

Insert the Windows Update function

Windows Update is a feature built into Windows, that gives you the latest updates for Windows and other Microsoft products, as an automatically providing.

1   To configure the settings for the Windows 8 Update, click Control Panel, click **System and Security – Windows Update**.

2   Click **Change settings** in the left pane.

3   If you do not want to worry about updates, select the option ❶ **Install updates automatically (recommended)**. To ensure that new updates are automatically downloaded and installed.

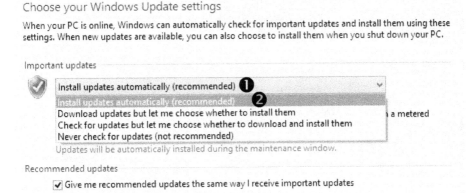

41

Keep your system up to date.

Tip! It's recommended as well to use the ❷ **Download updates** option, **but to choose the manual installation**. In order to be informed about new updates and choose when you want to install it.

Remove Troubleshooting a faulty patch

What can you do when a patch interferes with your system? One possibility is that you use the System Restore. The disadvantage of this method: All the other changes since the creation of the restore point will be lost. But you can also quickly uninstall the patch with these two steps:

1   On the Control Panel, click **Programs** and select the link **Programs and Features**.

2   Then click **View installed updates**.

3   Scroll down the bottom of the screen, where you will find the latest installed patch.

4   Click on the ❸ appropriate update and then ❹ **Uninstall**.

Here you installed patches and updates are displayed.

Tip! The patches are marked with a ❺ KB number. With this number you can search the Microsoft Support Center for further clues and solutions to this patch. You can find Microsoft's database for problem solving at: http://support.microsoft.com.

Find programs with secret internet access

Many programs take secret connection to the Internet. If you want to check what programs are currently accessing your PC to the Internet, follow these steps:

1 Press the key combination <**WIN**>+<**R**> and type ❶ **cmd**. Confirm with <**Return**>.

Go to the command line level.

2 In the command line enter ❷ **netstat -o** <**Return**>. You will now see a list of all current connections.

3 Note the ❸ PID number (Process Identification) of the processes that interest you.

You can display the current Internet connections.

4   Enable the Task Manager with the key combination
    <Ctrl>+<Alt>+<Delete> and click on the link **Task Manager**.

5   Click on the ❹ **Processes** tab. In the column with the ❺ PID numbers,
    you will now see, from the previously recorded PIDs, which process it is.

6   Should the missing record **PID** in Task Manager, click with the right
    mouse button in the column above line. For example, click next to the
    item **Status** and activate the ❻ PID entry in the context menu.

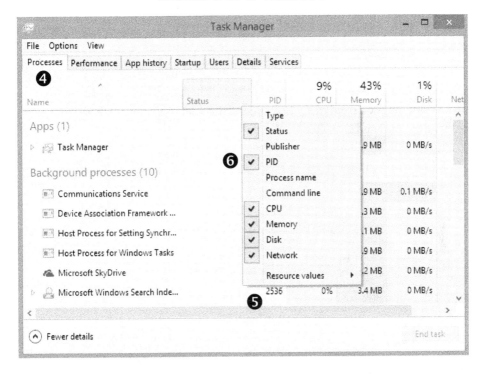

Identify the process by its unique PID (Process Identification).

Arrange your files to the standard program

Files are stored in folders on the hard drive. The name of a file consists of two parts: the file name and the file extension (an identifier consisting of three letters, which is separated by a dot on the file name). Based on the file type will be allocated to the respective programs. If you double-click in Windows Explorer, for example, a file will be opened with the associated program immediately.

Adjust the assignment of a file extension

But after a program change, the assignment of an extension of a program can change to another. Or you get the same error message, which says that there was no suitable program found for this file. When a file does not longer get opened by the requested program, you must correct the erroneous file association by hand:

1   Click the Windows-Explorer, right-click the ❶ file which association you want to change.

2   From the context menu click on ❷ **Open with**.

3   Select the entry ❸ **Choose default program**.

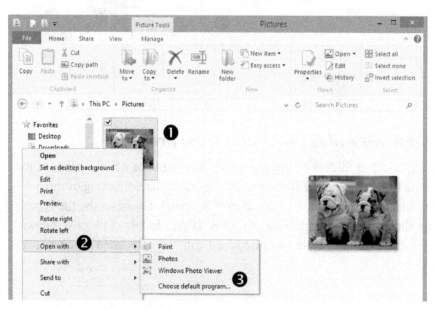

Select the file type association with the context menu.

46

4 Select from the list the program which should open the file

5 Highlight the requested selection ❹ application.

6 If the file henceforth should always be opened with this program, select
   the option ❺ **Use this app for all files**.

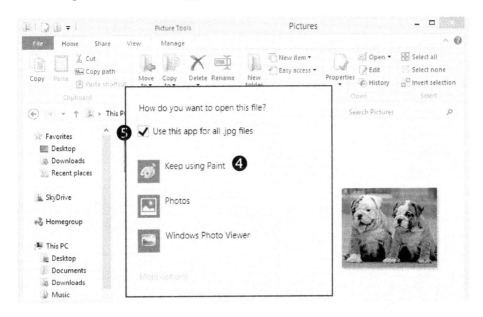

To change the file type association for your programs.

Remove crashed programs with the Resource Monitor

Although Windows 8 is very stable, but it happens that an application crashes
and freezes. Use Task Manager to terminate the affected application. Unsaved
data will mostly get lost, while this process.

So your data is retained

Therefore, try to finish the crashed process with the Resource Monitor. Then, the affected program remains in memory and you can save the changes in the open document as usual. Proceed as follows:

1   Enable the Task Manager with **<Ctrl>+<Alt>+<Delete>** and click the **Performance** tab.

2   Click on the link ❶ **Open Resource Monitor**.

3   Visit the **Overview** tab in which the **CPU** process is highlighted in red.

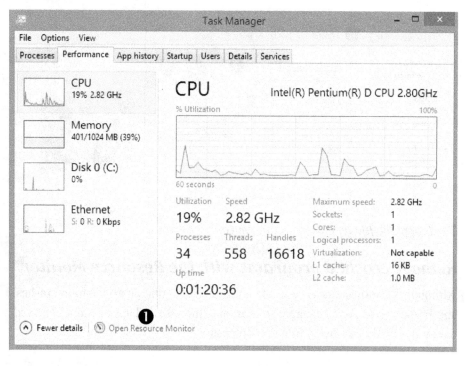

Enable the resource monitor via the Task Manager.

4   Click it with the right mouse button and select **Analyze Wait Chain**.

5   In the window which opens, you get all dependent on program processes and libraries displayed. You will also receive a description of why the program or dependent process stops responding.

6   Select the ❷ dependent process and click the ❸ **End Process** button.

7   In most cases, you can then continue to work with the program and save the unsaved data.

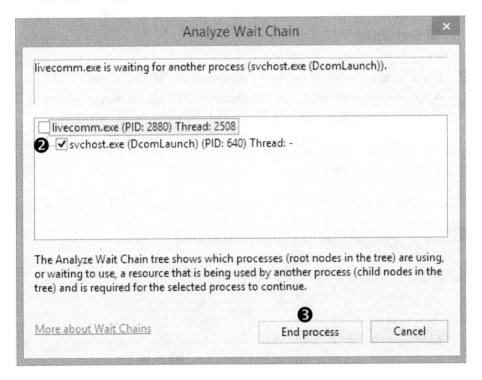

Cancel the dependent process, so that the problem is mostly done.

Analyze the cause of long starting times

If the startup takes a long time, which is usually due to auto-start programs. They mostly get unasked in the Startup folder and are automatically loaded at every system startup into memory.

Turn off the auto-start programs from

Use the system configuration, you can see the startup programs to display and switch off:

1   Enable the Task Manager with **<Ctrl>+<Alt>+<Delete>** and click on the ❶ **Startup** tab.

2   Disable unnecessary programs by removing the ❷ check mark. Alternatively, click on the **Disable** button to disable all startup programs. You must pre-select channels.

   Note: Security-related programs such as virus scanners activate automatically at the next start.

3   Perform a reboot in order to remove the startup programs from memory.

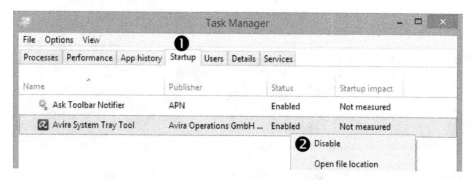

Disable for a long startup the startup programs.

Standard tools of Windows 8

If the system start now still take a very long time, you can analyze the start times of individual applications. To do this, insert the Event Viewer:

1   Start the Event Viewer with the key combination <**WIN**>+<**R**> and entering **eventvwr.msc**. Confirm by pressing <**Return**>.

2   Expand the folder and go to the entry ❸ **Application and Services Logs – Microsoft – Windows – Diagnostics-Performance – Operational**.

3   Entries with ❹ note **Critical** or those with Bug IDs from the value of 101, you should investigate further, as these indicate system faults.

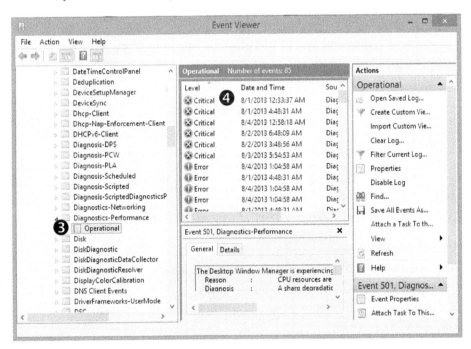

Select the Log of Windows 8.

51

4   To view more detailed ❺ information about an entry, double-click it.

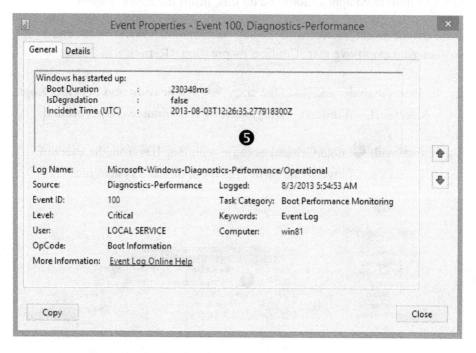

Let us show information about the error.

Rescue deleted files and old versions with the version history

To protect against data loss, you can enable the file version history on Windows 8. This function automatically backs up files and intermediate versions on a second hard drive or a USB stick. The disaster recovery is now done with a few clicks.

1   To enable the File Version History, press **<WIN>+<W>**.

2   Enter the text ❶ **file history** in the search field, and select the same ❷ entry.

Start the file version history of the settings.

3   Click on the link ❸ **Select Drive** and select the backup drive.

4   Click OK to confirm and activate the file version history by clicking on the button ❹ **Turn on**.

Select the backup drive.

5   From now on, Windows 8 now stores all the files and folders that are located in libraries, contacts, favorites, Microsoft SkyDrive or on the desktop.

Note: If you want to include additional folders in the backup, click on the folder to be backed up with the right mouse button and select **Add to Library**.

Tip! The backup every hour is activated by default. The interval you can customize with a click on **Advanced settings**. Select the option **Save copies of files** of the required period of time and confirm by clicking on **Save changes**.

In case of error, the data you provide the following to recover:

6   Press <WIN>+<W> and enter the text ❺ **restore files** in the search box

7   Click on ❻ **Restore your files with File History**.

8   Enter in the search box, select the file or use the arrow buttons to browse through your folders and files.

9   Select the desired data and click the **Restore** button.

Take advantage of the new features of Windows 8.

Tip! You can restore a file version in Windows-Explorer. Just click on the file and click in the group **Open** on the ❼ **History** button. There select the relevant version of the file or folder. Use the green round button to start the restore.

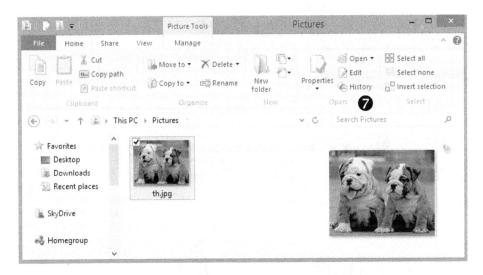

To adjust quickly restore a previous version.

Eliminate problems with an app

If an error occurs with an app, you will be notified by the Windows Store, Windows attempts to eliminate the problem. This usually solves the problem.

Update the app

If you continue to experience difficulties with an app, the subsequent step-by-step instructions will help you:

1   If you have problems with an app, you should update it first. Just click on the ❶ **Store** tile.

Enable the Windows Store.

2 Select in Charm menu the entry **Settings** (**<WIN>+<C>**).

3 Click on ❷ **App updates** and login if necessary with your Microsoft account.

Go to the settings.

4 Click on ❸ **Check for Updates**. If updates are available, click on **Select All** and click **Install**.

56

← App updates

Automatically update my apps

Yes

Automatic app updates isn't available when using a metered Internet connection.

Check for updates

Install the apps to the latest level.

5   If the problem persists, you should synchronize the app licenses. To do this, follow the above steps until step 3 and click on the button ❹ **Sync licenses**.

← App updates

Automatically update my apps

Yes

Automatic app updates isn't available when using a metered Internet connection.

Check for updates

App licenses

If you're not seeing up-to-date info for the apps you own, try syncing app licenses.

Sync licenses

Update the app licenses.

Otherwise with a defect app, usually only a new installation solves the problem. Just click on the relevant page of the app page with the right mouse button and select the bottom ❺ **Uninstall**.

Remove the app.

To install the app, click on the **Store** tile.

Click with the right mouse button on top of the screen and then click on **Your apps**.

Select the app to install and then click on ❻ **Install**.

Install the app on the store.

If you still have problems with the app, please contact the producer of the app. Click in the Windows-Store on the app and then click the index for more information or scroll to the right. Click on the ❼ Support link for the app.

Take advantage of the app vendor support.

Note: If problems occur not only at individual apps, but all apps are affected, you should clear the cache for the Windows Store. Press <**WIN**>+<**Q**> and enter in the search box the text ❽ **wsreset**. Click with the right mouse button on the eponymous icon and then click ❾ **Run as administrator**. Confirm the User Account Control message by clicking **Yes**, then the app cache is depleted.

Clean the cache server of the apps.

Tip! Some apps use a lot of ⑩ disk space. To find out the biggest memory hog, click the Charm menu (**<WIN>+<C>**) **Settings – Change PC settings - Search & apps – App sizes**.

Let us show the used space of the apps.

Create a Rescue Disk

Windows 8 provides many recovery features in case of emergency. You can enable this but only in a running system. If the system fails to start, you need the installation DVD of Windows 8. On this site you'll find analysis and recovery options. Simply create the installation DVD of Windows 8 in the drive and reboot the system. After selecting the language, select the point instead of installing computer repair options and troubleshooting.

If you do not have the installation DVD of Windows 8 next to you, you can also create a bootable USB stick or a CD with the recovery capabilities of Windows 8. This is done with a few mouse clicks:

1   Press the key combination <**WIN**>+<**X**> and select the **Control Panel** item.

2   Type in the search field the text ❶ **recovery**.

3   Click on the link ❷ **Create a recovery drive** and click **Next**.

Set the emergency of a rescue disk.

4   Insert a USB stick with a size of 256 MB. **Caution**: All data on the drive will be erased. Alternatively, you can also burn a CD.

5   To confirm that provide one-click **Create** and **Finish**.

Eliminate problems with hardware devices

Problems with hardware components you should check the connections and install the latest driver. Additionally, you can, as described below, use the Troubleshooting Windows 8:

Press <**WIN**>+<**X**> and select the **Control Panel** item.

Type in the search field the text ❶ **hardware** and click on the link ❷ **Find and fix problems with devices**.

61

Click the ❸ **Next** button and follow the wizard's instructions if necessary. In most cases, the troubleshooting faulty equipment automatically detects and restores. For mechanical damage, of course, only helps the replacement of that device.

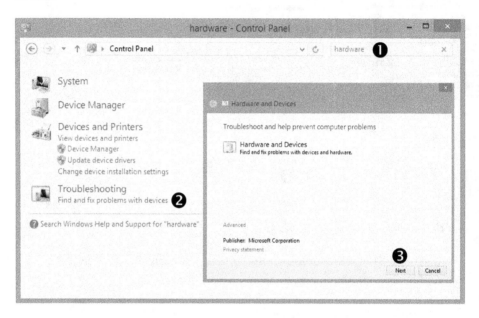

To eliminate interference from devices.

Tip! The troubleshooting, you can not only use for hardware problems, of course it can also help you system or Internet problems.

Use the troubleshooting on errors

Troubleshooting in Control Panel contains several repair programs that some common errors in the system can be resolved automatically, such as disturbances in networks, hardware and devices, the use of the Internet and program compatibility.

Get help with troubleshooting

To activate the troubleshooting, proceed as follows:

1   Activate the Control Panel and choose from **View by** the entry **Large icons**.

2   Click to **Action Center** and on the link ❶ Troubleshooting.

3   Select the ❷ Area and then the suitable solution from.

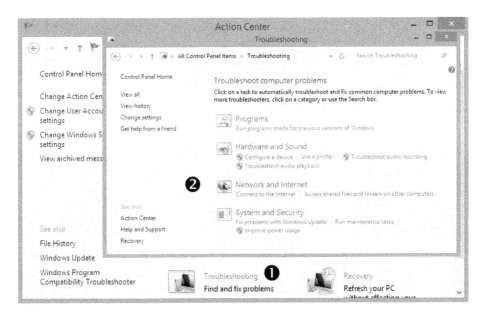

To solve system problems with troubleshooting.

4   When performing a troubleshooting you usually have to answer some questions or reset common settings, while the problem is resolved.

5   If the problem can't be solved, select among the displayed options. Then you will get more online troubleshooting information displayed.

Tip! Click the **Advanced** link in the troubleshooting and disable the option ❸ apply repairs automatically. After this, a list of solutions will be displayed for selection.

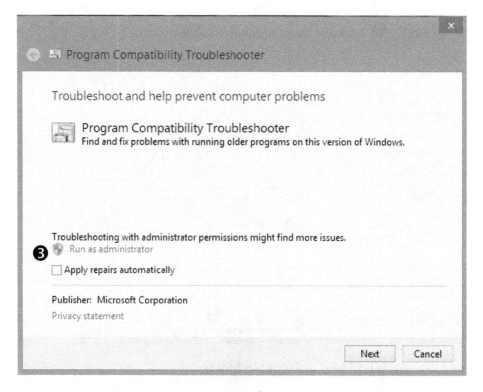

Let all solutions be displayed by clicking Next.

Let us show incorrect tools and programs

If software installations fail or programs crash, these events are logged on Windows 8. But through the reliability monitor, you can locate the programs that were involved responsible for any errors or crashes in the system.

Evaluate the reliability of the monitoring protocol

To use the reliability on monitoring system malfunctions proceed as follows:

1   Activate the Control Panel and choose from **View by** the entry **Large icons**.

2   Click on the link **Action center**.

3   Expand the service by clicking on the ❶ button with the arrow pointing up.

Check for system disorders Reliability Monitor in Windows 8.

4   Click on ❷ **View reliability history**.

Let the details be displayed to show the reliability.

5 If ❸ red dots are displayed in the following windows, you can also locate the defect application or program installation to the day exactly.

6 Just click on the item and look at the information in the lower pane. Click if offered, on the ❹ link **View solution** to fix the problem automatically.

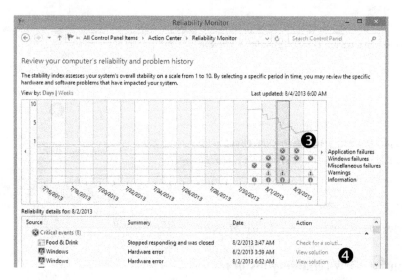

Windows 8 also usually offers a matching link to solve the problem.

Repair your applications automatically

Windows 8 offers the ability to automatically repair a program that has been damaged, for example due to a system error or deleted inadvertently. Many programs offer a useful function for such cases, which automatically checks, if all the necessary files and entries are still present in the registry, and possibly corrects errors. And so take advantage of this feature:

1   On the Control Panel click **Programs** and select the link **Programs and Features**.

2   Select the ❶ relevant application.

3   If this application offers a repair function, the ❷ **Repair** button displayed. Click this button and confirm the subsequent prompt.

4   Then the repair process is started and usually runs automatically. After a few seconds to a few minutes, the repair is complete, and you can work as usual with the application again.

Uninstall or change a program

To uninstall a program, select it from the list and then click Uninstall, Change or Repair.

Organise ▾ Uninstall Change Repair ❷	
Name	Publisher
7-Zip 9.21 ❶	Igor Pavlov
Adobe Reader XI (11.0.03) - Deutsch	Adobe Systems Incorporated
avast! Free Antivirus	AVAST Software
BrowserDefender	
CrystalDiskInfo 5.6.2	Crystal Dew World

67

Set your applications with just one click automatically.

How to ping with Windows 8 again

The firewall of Windows 8 evaluates a ping sometimes as enemy attack and therefore no longer responds to the ping command. So do the ICMP packets, you can cause with ping, but to:

1   To enable the firewall, press the key combination **<WIN>+<X>** and select **Control Panel**.

2   Click **System and Security** and select the link ❶ **Windows Firewall**.

Enable the user interface of the firewall.

3   In the left panel click on the link **Advanced Settings**.

4   Click on ❷ **Inbound Rules** and with the right mouse button on the entry ❸ **File and Printer Sharing (Echo Request - ICMPv4)**.

5   Select from the context menu the item ❹ **Enable rule**.

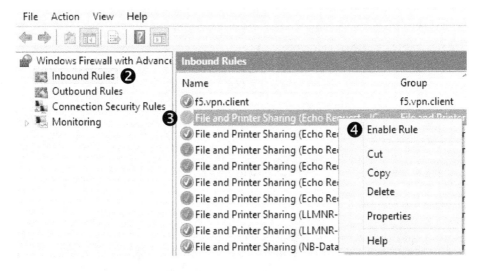

Immediately Windows 8 replies to pings again.

Restore the Hibernate

In Windows 8, it may happen that the Disk Cleanup works too thorough, for some users: not only unnecessary files are removed, but apparently also the whole hibernation mode. This happens whenever the Disk Cleanup also cleans up the scale from hibernation files and thus the hiberfil.sys file is removed. This file contains all the data are stored for hibernation. But you can easily put it to sleep again in a few steps:

1   Press the key combination **<WIN>+<X>** and select the entry ❶
Windows PowerShell (Admin).

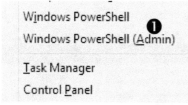

Windows PowerShell ❶
Windows PowerShell (Admin)

Task Manager
Control Panel

Start the command prompt with administrator privileges.

2   Then enter the Command ❷ **powercfg -h on** and press <**Return**> to enable hibernation.

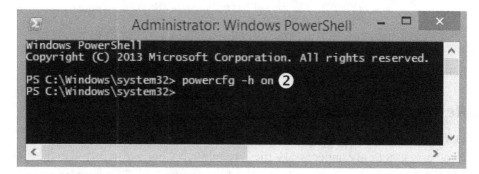

Restore the idle state of Windows 8.

Tip! If you want to shut down Windows 8 and the Hibernate option appears not in the menu charm: That's a problem, because all open documents and programs are stored on the hard disk and shut down the system. So you can continue your work with the familiar working environment at the next system startup. You should add **Hibernate** to the already existing options **Shut down** and **Restart** newly added:

1   Press <**WIN**>+<**W**> and enter the text ❶ **energy** in the search field.

2   Click on the entry ❷ **Power Options**.

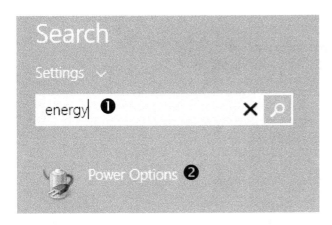

Activate the Power Options.

3   Click on the link ❸ **Choose what the power button does**.

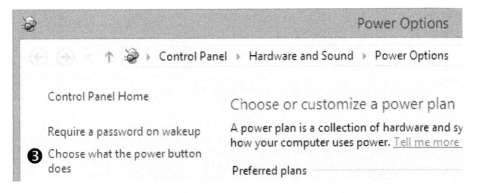

Configure the settings for the shutdown.

4   Click on the top of **Change settings that are currently unavailable**.

5   Check the bottom of ❹ **Hibernate –Show in Power menu**.

6   Confirm your selection by clicking on the **Save changes** button.

Shutdown settings

☑ **Turn on fast startup (recommended)**
This helps start your PC faster after shutdown.

❹ ☑ **Hibernate**
Show in Power menu.

☑ **Lock**
Show in account picture menu.

Get the Hibernate back into the Charm menu.

Remove malicious software with integrated virus scanner

If you suspect for viruses, you can examine the system in addition to the onboard Windows Defender Windows 8. This appears in Windows 8 now with the surface of the tested virus scanner Security Essentials.

1   Go to the home page and press the button ❶ with the down arrow.

Let us show all apps.

2   Click in the area **Windows system** on ❷ **Windows Defender**.

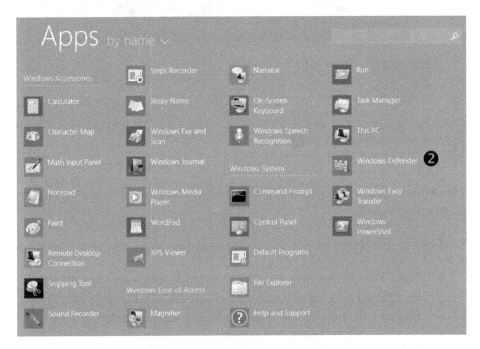

To start the integrated virus scanner for Windows 8.

3   Check whether the function ❸ **Real-time protection** is turned on. Real-time protection monitors all activities in the background and alerts you when a damaging program is active.

4   If real-time protection is turned off, click the **Settings** tab. Then put a check mark in front of the option **Turn on real-time protection (recommended)**.

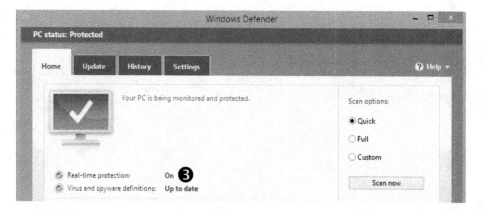

The onboard antivirus protects against viruses, worms and Trojans with a background guard.

5   Click on the **Home** tab and select the desired review:

- **Fast**: The Quick Check examines the areas, which are most likely to be infected by a harmful software. These include the programs, DLL libraries, the boot sector of the hard drive and the startup options.

- **Full**: For a complete review of all files on the disk and all current running programs get checked in memory. Depending on the system, the review may take longer than an hour.

- **Custom**: The custom scan, you can specify the storage media and folders, which are to be examined for viruses out.

6   Select the scan by clicking on the ❹ **Scan Now** button.

7   Then the system is analyzed for a damaging software.

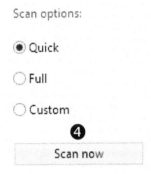

Test the system for viruses.

Adjust the visual effects individually to

The visual effects of Windows 8 are indeed a true eye-catcher, but they require strong graphics card and processor. If something takes after a few seconds after a mouse click, you should maybe reduce the visual effects and thereby increase system performance again.

1 Click with the right mouse button on the start button and open the ❶ **Control Panel**.

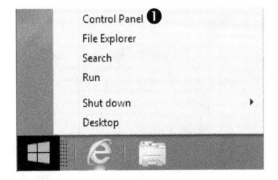

Activate the context menu of the start button.

2   Choose from **View by** the entry ❷ **Large icons**.

3   Click on the link ❸ **System** and then top left, click **Advanced system settings**.

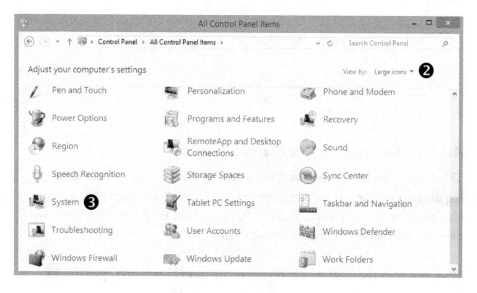

Let us show the advanced system settings.

4   Select the **Advanced** tab and the **Settings** button in the **Performance** area.

5   Activate the option ❹ **Adjust for best performance** to turn off the visual effects.

6   About the option **Custom** to set the visual effects individually.

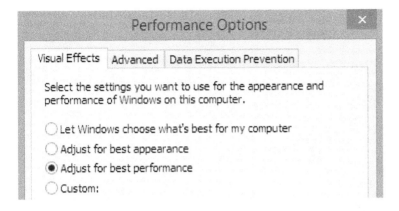

To turn off all unnecessary visual effects.

Check the RAM for errors

My system was always running perfectly so far, but for a short time unexplained crashes appear again and again? There could be a defect memory module to blame for this. With the memory diagnosis, which is built into Windows 8, you can check this easily.

1   Start the Control Panel and choose from **View by** the entry **Large icons**.

2   Click **Administrative Tools** and double-click the entry ❶ **Windows Memory Diagnostic**.

3   You can now get the option to either memory test ❷ make immediately or at the next system startup.

4   After the system restarts, the diagnosis of your system memory begins. Of the progress and any error while you are fully informed.

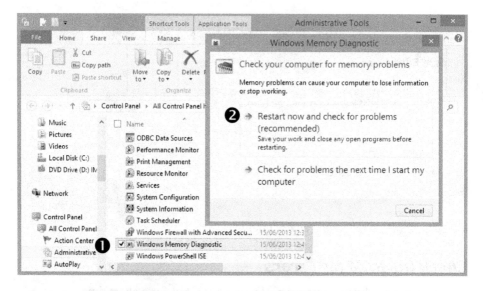

Check the memory, if sporadic crashes appear.

Check for errors access permissions

If a message is displayed, while opening a file, that access has been denied, proceed as follows:

1   Click with the right mouse button on the file or folder and select **Properties** from the context menu.

2   Click the **Security** tab and click on your ❶ name, to determine what ❷ permissions you have on the system.

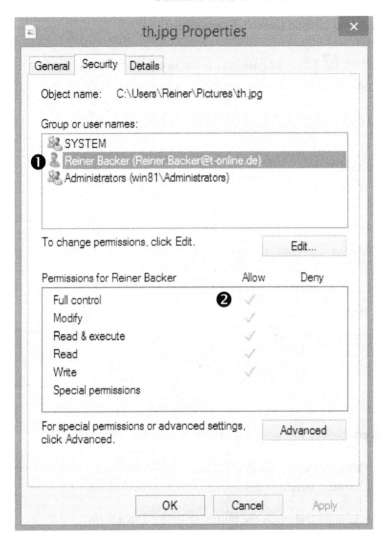

Let your permissions be displayed to you.

In addition, check if the file is encrypted. Proceed as follows:

1   Click the **General** tab and then click **Advanced**.

2   Is the check box ❸ **Encrypt contents to secure data enabled**, you are required to open the file, with the certificate which it was encrypted.

If the content is encrypted, you need a certificate to access the document.

Tip! Windows 8 includes a troubleshooting wizard that provides an interactive solution to the selected problem:

1   Go to the home page and press the button with the down arrow.

2   Click in the area **Windows system** on **Help and Support**.

3   Enter ❶ keywords in the search box to the problem and select the ❷ corresponding entry.

Standard tools of Windows 8

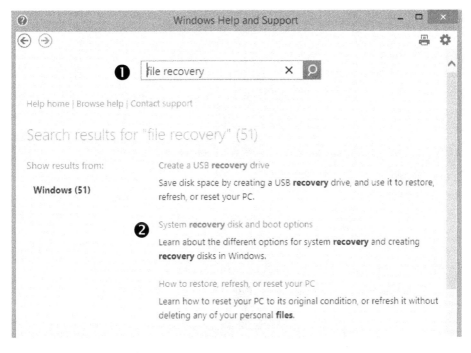

Windows 8 includes a troubleshooting wizard.

Driver Troubleshooting

If your system will not boot or crashes regularly, the native Windows system functions are often the last resort. Then a start in safe mode is usually still possible. You can then reset your system, for example, with the system restore to a stable state.

Search for driver problems in Device Manager

If drivers cause problems, Windows sometimes reacts very sensitive. A look at the on-board device manager here quickly brings clarity about the cause of the error. There you will find extensive information about your hardware and also information on possible driver error.

1   To activate the Device Manager, press the key combination
    <WIN>+<Pause>. Click on the link ❶ **Device Manager**.

Activate the Device Manager of Windows 8.

82

Driver Troubleshooting

2   To display additional buttons, select a device. For example, expand the entry **Display adapters** and click on the ❷ entry below.

3   Click ❸ here to search for new/changed hardware.

4   A click on this ❹ icon updated the driver for the selected device.

5   Click ❺ here to remove the selected device.

6   A click on this ❻ icon disables the device.

7   To get more details about a driver file, click on the relevant driver entry with the right mouse button. Then select the entry ❼ **Properties**, go to the **Driver** tab and click on the button ❽ **Driver Details**.

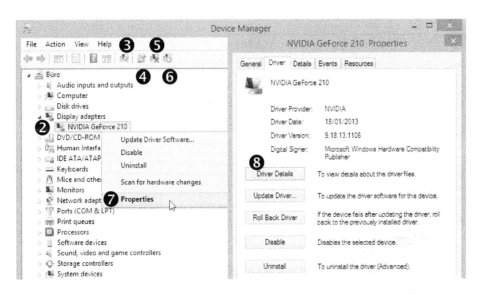

The Device Manager in Windows 8.

Driver Troubleshooting

If a component is not properly installed, this will be displayed in the Device Manager with a warning:

Warning	Statement
? Yellow question mark	With a big yellow question mark Windows indicates components that were correctly detected by Windows, but for which no drivers are installed. In this case, install the latest driver from the producer of your device. Just click on the entry with the right mouse button and select **Update Driver Software**.
X Red Cross	With a red cross Windows indicates components that are disabled. If you have just reinstalled the device, restart your system to let Windows detect the device. If you have the component disabled, click the **Enable** icon in the top right of the Device Manager.
! Black exclamation mark on a yellow background	Critically, however, is the yellow error symbol with an exclamation mark ("!"). Windows does not recognize the device and therefore can't access it. What kind of problem it is, will be explained by the Device Manager. Just double click that entry. In most cases, the cause is a defect or unsuitable driver.

8   To fix the error, double-click the warning icon.

9   The **Device status** box usually tells you more information about the problem.

10 After clicking the **Troubleshoot** button, Windows 8 will also help you in fixing it, by showing you exemplary solutions for simple error types.

Driver Troubleshooting

11 In addition, you should install the latest drivers for, in the Device Manager with a warning note marked, hardware components.

If something is wrong with your PC Hardware, Device Manager displays an error code. Below you will find the most important error codes with the matching solution:

Code	Notification	Solution
1	The device is not configured correctly, because the hardware detection failed.	This code means that Windows can not configure the device. To solve the problem, follow the instructions in the **Device Status** box. If the error is not cleared, delete the device from the Device Manager and then try a clean install with the hardware wizard. Also, a driver update can help.
3	Device driver is corrupted or memory or resource shortage.	Update the driver for the first device. If this does not solve the problem, remove the device from Device Manager and reinstall it. Check the memory and system resources of your device.
8	The unit does not work because the driver file is corrupted <Name>.	Click **Update Driver Software**.
10	Device not present, not working properly or driver is not installed.	Make sure that the device is properly connected. If there is no problem with the connection, update the driver.

18	Driver must be installed.	The driver is damaged, please update the driver.
23	The problem is with the graphics card.	Remove the graphics card from the Device Manager and restart your PC. Update the video card driver.
24	Device not available.	Hardware fault, or there is a need of a new driver.

Browse the system log for defect drivers

If the problem can not be solved by updating the driver, examine the Event Viewer System log:

1   Press **<WIN>+<X>** and select the entry **Control Panel**.

2   Click **System and Security – Administrative Tools** and double-click on the entry ❶ Event Viewer.

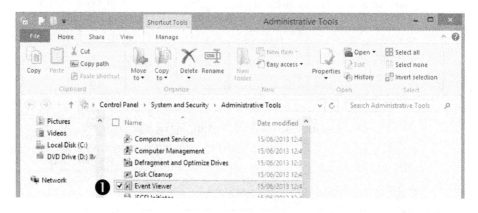

Start the Event Viewer from the Control Panel.

Driver Troubleshooting

3   In the left part of the window click on ➋ **Windows Logs**.

4   Click on the entry ➌ **System** to have a look at the system log. In this protocol, you can find events that have been logged by the Windows system components. Here Error loading a device driver or startup errors are recorded in connection with other system components, for example.

5   Click on ➍ **Level** and then scroll back to the top of the window to display all errors at the top of the list.

6   Browse the entries that are marked as errors. If you are under ➎ **Source** make an entry to a driver, double click on this entry. You will then receive further information about the driver, which you should renew.

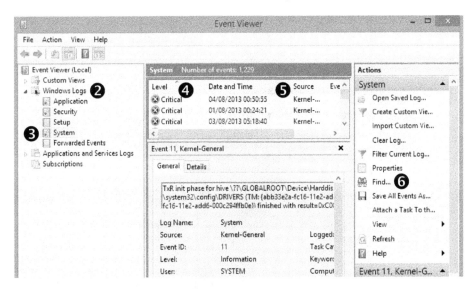

Windows 8 stored in the system log messages that are caused by drivers or services.

Tip! Check the ❻ search function and browse additionally the system log for entries that contain the text include ❼ **driver**.

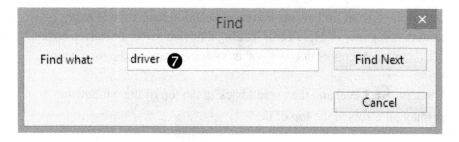

Use the search function for error analysis.

Use the Driver Info Center for Windows

Windows 8 contains the program information system to search for driver errors. To start the tool, press **<WIN>+<R>**. Type **msinfo32** and press **<Return>**.

1   In the section **System Summary**, you can find the folder **Hardware Resources** with the entry ❶ **Conflicts/Sharing**. I a new device, which does not function, uses the same resources as another device, you have found the error.

2   In the folder **Components** you will find the helpful entry ❷ **Problem Devices**. Therein any existing devices are listed without a ❸ proper driver connection.

3   In the folder **Software Environment** the entry ❹ **System Drivers** will be helping you. Here you will find the name of the driver and the

associated file name, the start state and mode of the individual driver and other information.

Through the system-information you will find everything worth knowing about the system drivers.

Check out the unsigned drivers in your system

Windows 8 checks during the installation, if a device driver from Microsoft has been tested and is digitally signed. If this is not the case, you will receive a warning message during the installation.

Non-Microsoft signed drivers are many and most also work flawlessly. But unsigned drivers can also be the cause of a system failure. So it pays to check what unsigned drivers installed on your system:

1 Press **<WIN>+<R>**, type the command **sigverif** and press **<Return>**.

2 Enable the driver check by clicking on ❶ **Start**.

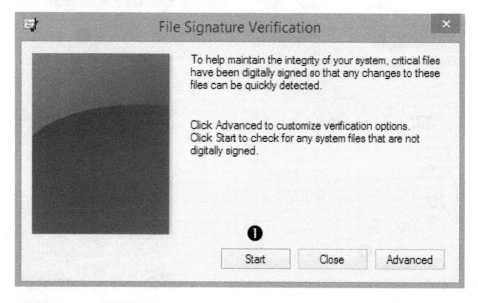

Determine the unsigned drivers in your system.

3 After about a minute all of your unsigned drivers are displayed. Most
   drivers have the file extension *. SYS or *. DRV.

Search for the, as problematic signed drivers in the list, for drivers on the
producer's websites, which have been signed by Microsoft. Install this driver
instead.

Use the latest driver for your graphics card

If you have problems with your graphics card, you should first update the
graphics card driver. To do this, use the driver for the chip producer of the
card. This driver offers you usually the best performance and additional

Driver Troubleshooting

features. To find out which version your driver has, use the DirectX Diagnostic Tool:

1   Press <**WIN**>+<**R**>, enter **dxdiag** and press <**Return**>. Confirm the security prompt by clicking **Yes**.

2   Click the tab ❶ **Display** and check the ❷ date of the current driver.

3   The tool automatically tests your graphics system and tells you ❸ possible graphics problems.

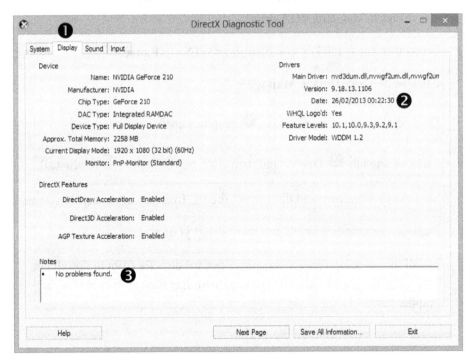

View the date from your graphics card driver.

91

Tip! But even if your graphics system is stable, you should upgrade your graphics card driver every two months. This is especially important if you are using complex 3D applications. Because by a driver update, you eliminate errors in the display of textures and get free new functions.

Fix Driver margins when changing the graphics card

There are often problems when a new graphics card replaces an older model. This is especially the case if the new graphics card is equipped with a different GPU type than the previous model. Therefore delete the driver before replacing your old graphics card. Windows then sets instead of vendor-specific driver to standard VGA driver.

1   To do this, press the key combination <**WIN**>+<**Pause**>.

2   Click on the link **Device Manager**.

3   Double-click the entry for your ❶ graphics card.

4   Click on the tab ❷ **Driver** and then click on the button ❸ **Uninstall**.

5   Shut down Windows and disconnect the PC from the power supply system.

6   Replace the graphics board and then restart your system.

7   Install the latest drivers for the graphics card directly from the producer. This usually offers a separate package with Installation Wizard for the graphics card.

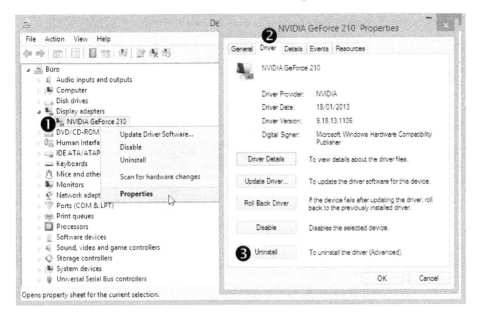

Remove the graphics card driver by using Device Manager.

Solve STOP errors, which are caused by defect driver

Damaged or incorrect programmed drivers solve most of a Stop error that is displayed in the form of a blue screen. Windows stops with a blue screen, then nothing works. The Windows kernel has detected a situation that he can not fix without any data loss or system inconsistencies.

The kernel responds to this state of emergency by a „bug check", your system stops specific and then gives you a blue screen with an error message in white written notes on the problem encountered. Before it comes to the actual stop, the system can also save a memory dump to a file for further analysis.

The ❶ Blue Screen in Windows 8 looks somewhat benevolent than the previous versions. But all unsaved data are also gone for the first time. A clue for the cause of the system crash you will get with Windows 8, only in the form of an ❷ Error message (Bug Check String). Important information such as the error code or the parameters are mostly missing completely.

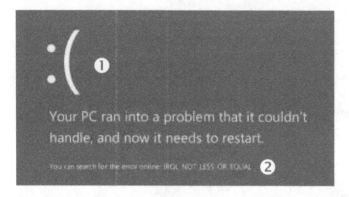

A blue screen in Windows 8.

Use with Windows 8 the tool **BlueScreenView** (www.nirsoft.net). This shows details of the induced blue screen. Find the details below by the ❸ Bug Check String and Bug Check Code with Google.

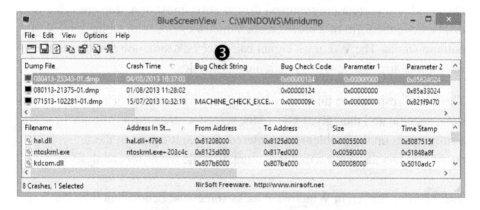

*Analyze the cause of the blue screen with **BlueScreenView**.*

Driver Troubleshooting

Note: If the tool does not provide information on a blue screen, check in the Control Panel under **System and Security – System – ❹ Advanced System Settings – Startup and Recovery – ❺ Settings**, that the blue screen is ❻ entered in the system log (default).

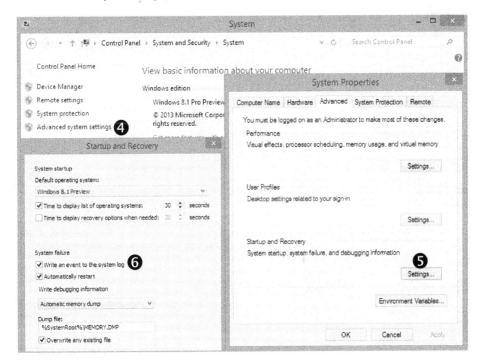

Check the start-up and restore settings.

Tip! When a STOP error occurs, you should first restore your system to the last working system configuration. If the error occurs during system startup, select Safe Mode to.

Stop errors are caused by driver error to 90%. Note the error code in the right part of the error message. The codes refer to a driver error:

Driver Troubleshooting

Error text	Description
CM_PROB_ NOT_ CONFIGURED	No driver available
CM_PROB_FAILED_ START	Defect device driver
CM_PROB_PARTIAL_ LOG_CONF	Defect hardware or defect device driver
CM_PROB_UKNOWN_ RESOURCE	Defect or invalid device driver
CM_PROB_FAILED_ INSTALL	Corrupt drivers Readme
PROCESS_HAS_LOCKED_PAGES	Incorrect driver
NO_MORE_SYSTEM_PTES	Incorrect driver
IRQL_NOT_LESS_OR_EQUAL	Incorrect or damaged hardware driver
KMODE_EXCEPTION_NOT_HANDLED	defect driver

The error codes will give you information about the type of driver error – to correct this, install a new driver.

Printer problems resolved quickly

If the printer is technically fine and Windows 8 still does not print, there often begins a tedious trouble hunting. After checking the controls, cables and paper stock, a system problem is the only remaining possibility.

Insert the Print Advisor

A time-consuming and complicated troubleshooting can be avoided if you take the Print Advisor to complete. The Print Advisor interactively guides you with step-by-step solutions to the printing problem:

1   Activate the Control Panel (**<WIN>+<X>**) and choose from **View by** the entry **Large icons**.

2   Click on **Action Center** and on the link **Troubleshooting**.

3   Click the link ❶ **Use a Printer** and in the next window click on ❷ **Next**.

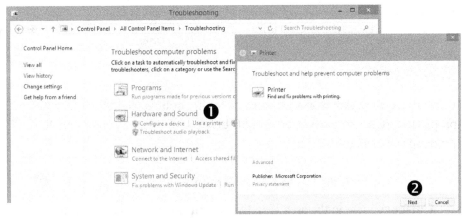

Analyze the error with the Print Advisor.

4   Then the problem is analyzed

5   Click on ❸ **Try these repairs as an as Administrator**.

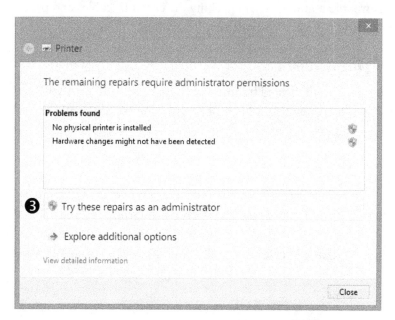

Let's solve the problem with the printer from the system.

Reinstall the printer driver

If the above Print Advisor is no solution to the problem and the printer properties are set properly, you should solve the problem by removing the printer driver and reinstall it.

1   To do this, open the Control Panel (**<WIN>+<X>**) and click in the ❹ **Category** view in the area **Hardware and Sound** on ❺ **View devices and printers**.

Printer problems resolved quickly

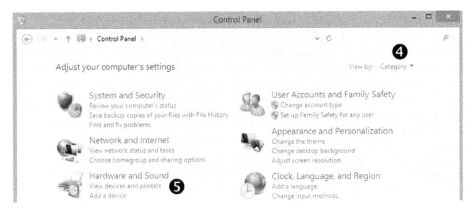

You can view the installed printer.

2 Click with the right mouse button on the printer you want to remove and select the entry ❻ **Remove device.**

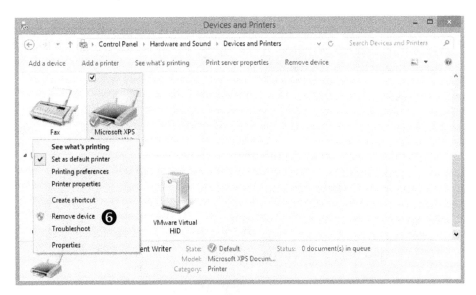

Remove the printer driver with the context menu.

Set up the printer using the installation wizard

If your printer has a USB port, the printer should be automatically recognized and installed when connecting from Windows. If not, you must install the printer manual. Just follow the following step-by-step guide:

1 Activate the Control Panel (**<WIN>+<X>**) and enter in the **Search**-field the text **printer**.

2 Click on **Devices and Printers** and ❶ **add a printer**.

Use the printer installation wizard.

3 Choose, in the Wizard, the point a local printer.

4 Specify the connection and click **Next**.

5 Select **Install the printer driver**, the printer model and click **Next**.

  • If your printer is not listed, click **Windows Update** and wait while Windows looks for additional drivers.

100

- If no printers are available and you have the installation CD, browse to the folder where the printer driver is stored.

6 Follow the wizard and click **Finish**.

Search for driver problems in Device Manager

The printing process is handled via the Windows spooler service (print queue). This service must be activated, or printing is not possible and you receive the error message that the service has not been started.

1 To check whether the service is enabled, proceed as follows:

2 Press **<WIN>+<X>** and select the entry **Control Panel**. In the **Search** box type **services**.

3 Click on the link ❶ **View Local Services**.

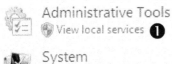

Administrative Tools
  View local services ❶

System
  Allow remote access to your computer
  Allow Remote Assistance invitations to be sent from this computer
  Invite someone to connect to your PC and help you, or offer to help someone else
  Select users who can use remote desktop

Let the local services be shown to you.

4 Double-click on the service ❷ **Print Spooler**.

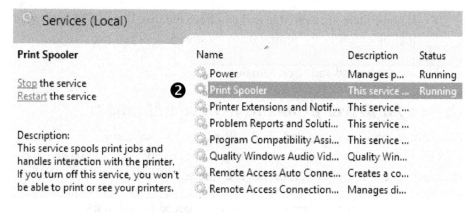

Let the properties of the print queue be shown to you.

5   Set the Startup type to ❸ **Automatic** and enable the service if it is stopped.

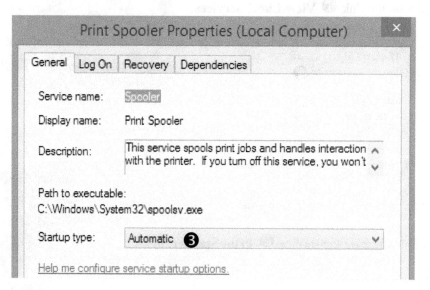

Ensure that the spooler service is started.

Check the settings in the BIOS

If your new printer or other external device strikes, there could possibly something be set wrong in the BIOS. Therefore, check in the menu **Integrated Peripherals** or **Advanced - I / O Device Configuration** the settings.

Tip! To activate the BIOS Setup, press depending on the BIOS manufacturer during PC boot of the following keys: <**F1**>, <**Del**>, <**Control**>+<**Alt**>+<**Esc**> or <**Ctrl**>+<**Esc**>. What is the key, is displayed at startup.

- **Onboard Parallel Port**: Ask here **Auto** or **378/IRQ7**. The default address of the first parallel port LPT1 is 378h, LPT2 is set to 278h.

CMOS Setup Utility - Copyright © 1984-2006 Award Software I/O Device Configuration		
Onboard Serial Port	[Auto]	Item Help
Onboard Parallel Port	[Auto]	Menu Level ▶
Parallel Port Mode	[ECP]	
USB Device	[Enabled]	BIOS can automatically Configure all the
USB Keyboard Support	[Enabled]	Boot and Plug and Play Compatible devices.
OnChip 1394	[Auto]	If you cannot select IRQ
Infrared-Port	[Auto]	DMA and memory base Adress fields, since
Onboard 6Ch H/W Audio	[Enabled]	BIOS automatically
Joystick	[Enabled]	Assigns them
Move Enter: Select +/-/PU/PD:Value		F10:Save ESC:Exit
F1:General Help F5:Previus Values		F7: BIOS Setup Defaults

Here you will find the BIOS options for your interfaces.

103

- **USB Device**: This setting should be set to **Enabled** to use the USB ports on your motherboard.

- **OnChip 1394**: Here you can configure the onboard FireWire port. To enable this, set the option to **Auto**.

Checklist: Getting Help When Things Go Wrong

Often the causes of a problem with the printer are trivial, using the following checklist will help you to find the cause quickly:

- Is the power cord to the printer connected?

- If the printer and computer are turned on?

- Is the USB cable connected to the printer and to the computer?

- Printer lights blinking and the display will show a warning? See the printer manual.

- If ink printers: Did you remove the sticker and tape from the back and bottom of the cartridges?

- Laser printers: Do you have the protective film on the output of the toner cartridge removed?

- Is the paper loaded correctly? Make sure that the paper is not too far into the printer.

- Is the printer set as the default printer? If not, set the printer as the default:

Printer problems resolved quickly

1   Go to the Control Panel and enable the printer dialog.

2   Click with the right mouse button on the printer and make sure that the
option is set ❶ **Set as default printer**.

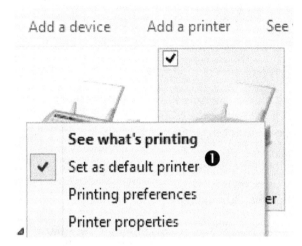

Determine the default printer.

Registry-Troubleshooting

The registration database (registry) of Windows 8 is used as a central point for collecting all system-specific settings. It stores information about the hardware configuration, settings, programs and user settings to desktop and Start menu. You are right there, if you want to configure Windows individually and eliminate persistent system disorders.

To start the Registry Editor

To make the registry settings, which were presented in this chapter, you need the Windows registry editor. To not describe the registry-settings on every start of the tool again, this can be done at this point.

To start the Registry Editor, follow these steps:

1   Press **<WIN>+<R>** to display the **Run** dialog.

2   In the Open box type ❶ **regedit** and click on ❷ **OK**. If necessary, confirm the safety message by clicking **Yes**.

Start Registry Editor from the ***Run*** *dialog.*

106

Eliminate delays when starting the program

If programs start after a short delay, you can change that with an intervention in the registry.

1   Navigate to the key HKEY_CURRENT_USER \ Software \ Microsoft \ Windows \ CurrentVersion \ Explorer.

2   Under **Explorer** create the key **Serialize**. Just click on **Explorer** and select **Edit – New – Key**.

3   Click with the right mouse button in the right pane and select ❶ **New – DWORD (32-bit) Value**.

4   Assign for the entry the name ❷ **StartupDelayInMSec** and leave the value at **0**.

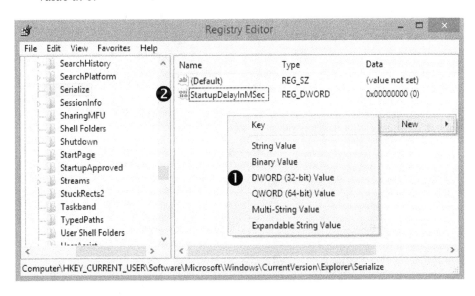

Accelerate the program start with an engagement in the registry.

After installing the DVD, let the drive be shown again

In older DVD drives, it is possible that these will not be longer displayed after the installation of Windows 8. To resolve the problem, proceed as follows:

1   Navigate to the key HKEY_LOCAL_MACHINE \ SYSTEM \ CurrentControlSet \ Services \ atapi \ Controller0.

2   If in the right half of the window the entry ❸ **EnumDevice1** misses, insert it in new.

3   Assign to the entry the value ❹ **1** and click **OK**.

4   Restart the system, now the DVD drives should be displayed again.

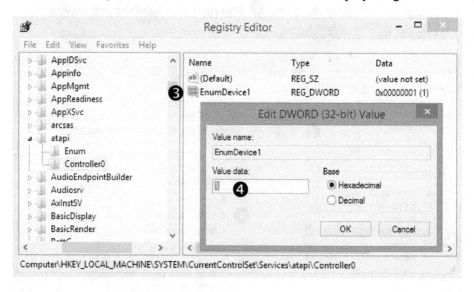

Bind older ATAPI drives in the file system.

108

Eliminate duplicate links on the desktop

When you create a desktop shortcut, this sometimes appears in duplicate. You will see two icons with the same name. But behind it there are obviously not two different files. Because if you look at the properties, both links show the same path. In addition, the links disappear again in pairs, if you just delete one of them. To correct the problem:

1 Navigate to the key ❺ HKEY_LOCAL_MACHINE \ SOFTWARE \ Microsoft \ Windows \ CurrentVersion \ Explorer \ User Shell Folders.

2 Double-click in the right pane of the entry **Common Desktop** and assign it to ❻ **% PUBLIC%\Desktop**.

3 Reboot your system, to make one icon appearing for a shortcut.

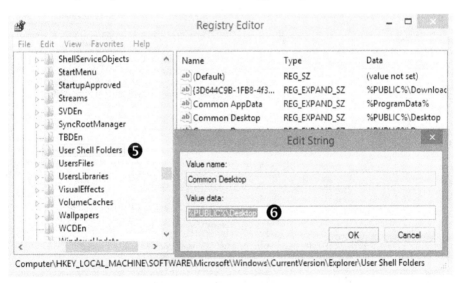

To solve the desktop chaos with the double icons.

Seal the Explorer window of each other

If you have multiple windows opened in Windows Explorer or Internet Explorer, and then explorer then crashes, the windows will all be closed. You can prevent this, if you assign any Explorer window a separate process. To enable the function:

1   Go to the key ❼ HKEY_CURRENT_USER \ Software \ Microsoft \ Windows \ CurrentVersion \ Explorer \ Advanced.

2   Create the entry ❽ **SeparateProcess** (DWORD (32-Bit) value) if it does not already exist. Assign it a value of **1**.

3   In a crash, then only the relevant Explorer window is closed.

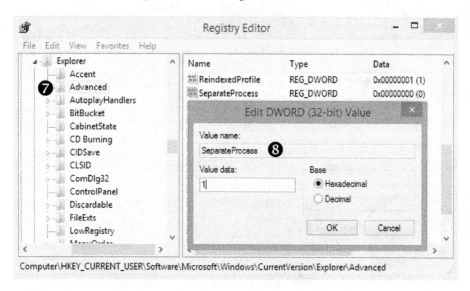

Allot Windows and Internet Explorer to its own process.

Tip! Set the value to **0** or simply delete the value, if you want to put a change in the registry back to the default.

Bind the Bluetooth device back into your system

On Windows, there can be problems with your Bluetooth devices. Either they are not recognized properly, services do not work or you can not connect to the devices. To remedy this:

1   Go to the 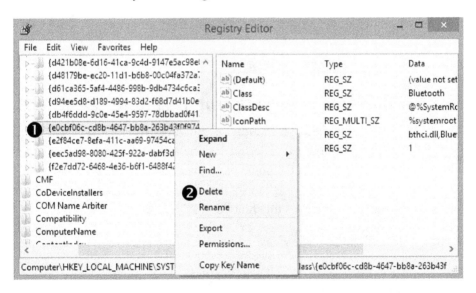 key HKEY_LOCAL_MACHINE \ SYSTEM \ CurrentControlSet \ Control \ Class \ {e0cbf06c-CD8b-4647-bb8a-263b43f0f974}.

2   Click on the entry with the right mouse button and ❷ delete it.

Delete the Bluetooth entry in the registry.

3   Press **<WIN>+<Pause>** and click on **Device Manager**.

4   Highlight the entry Bluetooth of that device and delete it.

5   Select ❸ **Action – Scan for hardware changes** and reinstall the
    Bluetooth drivers.

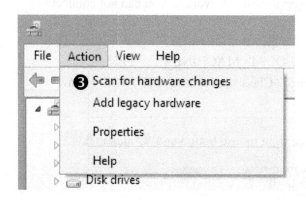

Remove and reinstall the Bluetooth drivers.

Repair redirected page in the Internet Explorer

The manipulation of the Internet Explorer is growing in popularity with
providers of mostly dubious offers. After visiting a page, this gets simply
added, without requesting, as the home page. By clicking on Tools - Internet
Options in Internet Explorer, you can set the requested website in the Home
While up again. But sometimes this function has been blocked.

To restore the default page, you have to remove some keys from the registry:

1   Navigate to the key HKEY_CURRENT_USER \ Software \ Microsoft \
    Internet Explorer \ Main.

2   In the right window look for the entries ❹ **Search Bar**, **Search Page** and **Start Page**.

3   If available, click the right mouse button on the entries and ❺ delete this. There don't have to be all of the above entries. Just delete the ones that are available.

4   Thus, the usual home site and the setting functions are activated again on the Home.

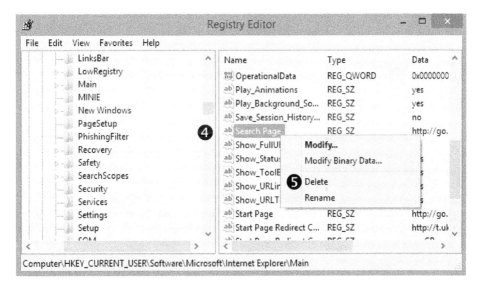

Restore the usual categories.

So your applications can reinstall

If the installation routine suddenly freezes when installing an application, this is usually caused by an incorrect setting in the registry. To correct the setting and bring the Windows Installer back on track, follow these steps:

1   Go to the key ❻ HKEY_CURRENT_USER \ Software \ Microsoft \ Windows \ CurrentVersion \ Explorer \ Shell Folders.

2   Double-click on the entry ❼ **Recent** and enter the path ❽ **C:\Users\\<*username*>\AppData\Roaming\Microsoft\Windows\Recent** in the field. The entry **<username>** is the currently logged on user on the system.

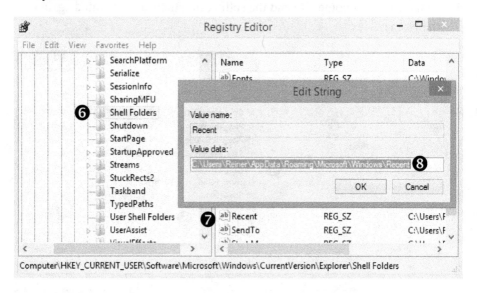

Repair the Windows Installer through a small intervention in the registry.

Remove deleted programs from the software list

In the Control Panel you will see under **Programs** all installed ❶ applications.

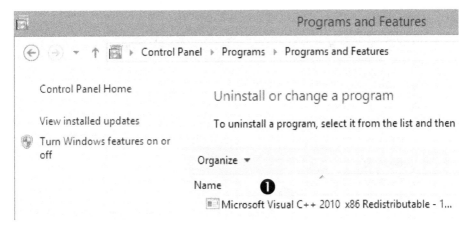

In the Control Panel, see the Windows 8 installed programs.

If the uninstallation of a program is not working properly, it may be that the Windows application there still performs, although it is no longer available.

This can happen when you delete an application's files from the Explorer or the uninstall routine was aborted with an error. Such a defect software entry can be removed quickly, just through a small intervention in the registry:

1   Navigate to the key HKEY_LOCAL_MACHINE \ SOFTWARE \ Microsoft \ Windows \ CurrentVersion \ Uninstall.

2   Each ❷ subkey is here for a program that is displayed in the Control Panel under Programs.

3   Search for the name of the application and click on it with the right mouse button.

4   Select ❸ **Delete** and make sure that the application is no longer displayed under Programs in the Control Panel.

115

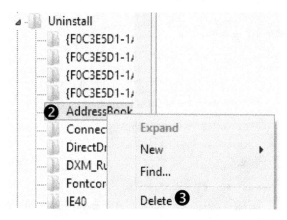

How to remove Windows 8 entries in the channel list manually.

Remove the entries from the integrated search

If you click in the integrated search of Windows on the input field with the left mouse button, it displays all the keywords that you entered previously. You can delete individual entries in the search by clicking with the mouse on the item and press the **Delete** key.

You can also remove the entries from the Windows Registry:

1 Navigate to the key: HKEY_CURRENT_USER \ Software \ Microsoft \ Windows \ CurrentVersion \ Explorer \ WordWheelquery.

2 Click the Key **WordWheelquery** with the right mouse button and select the entry **Delete**.

3 Confirm the deletion of the above mentioned key with a click on **Yes**.

116

Professional tools for troubleshooting and data recovery

The searching for configuration or hardware errors is often a complex and time-consuming task, which you nearly can't accomplish without analysis tools. If your PC is still starting, you can use the tools on the following pages for effective fault analysis and data recovery. And the best: Good analysis, repair and data recovery tools don't need to be expensive. All tools presented below are freeware, and therefore will cost you nothing. These programs can be the most expensive full versions in every way.

How to retrieve deleted files from the Recycle Bin

A click on the button <**Del**> and the selected file in Windows-Explorer or in a program file menu is deleted and moved to the Windows Recycle Bin. From the Recycle Bin, you can restore the files easily or permanently delete them:

1   To restore a file, double click on the icon **Recycle Bin** on the desktop.

2   Highlight the ❶ desired file or group.

3   Click on the object with the right mouse button and select ❷ **Restore**.

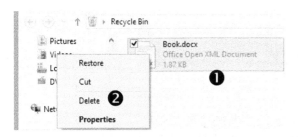

Recover deleted files from Recycle Bin.

117

Professional tools for troubleshooting and data recovery

Tip! If working with files, such as Windows Explorer don't work out with something – there is no reason for concern. Almost all Windows programs and tools are equipped with an UNDO function, which can undo all performed operations in several steps.

Multiple stages mean that if you have deleted a file, for example first and then moved another file in another folder, you would press the Undo button twice to make the erase and undo the move operation. By pressing <**Ctrl**>+<**Z**> the UNDO function is triggered in almost all Windows tools and programs.

Deleted files are still available on the hard disk

If a deleted file has been removed from the Recycle Bin, it can not be recovered with the standard tools of Windows. But you don't need to give up about this lost file yet. There are utilities that can reconstruct deleted files.

These programs make use of the fact that Windows deletes files. While deleting the data, which are stored in this file, these are still retained. Windows simply marks the space occupied by the deleted file as free. As long as this space has not been overwritten by new data, you can restore the deleted file.
How safely the deleted files can be recovered depends on several factors:

- How much time has passed since the deletion? The longer ago the deletion date, the more likely Windows has already allocated the memory and the data are otherwise irretrievably lost.

- How big is the file to be recovered? The recovery prospects are much better than large files with small files.

- If you have started a defrag after deleting the file? Then sectors of the deleted file might have been moved and can not be saved.

Rescue deleted files with Recuva

Have you accidentally deleted important files and already emptied the Recycle Bin, they can save in this situation, the data recovery tool **Recuva** (www.piriform.com/recuva).

The restoration works with all types of media, whether MP3 player, USB stick, memory card or hard drive. For this the tool will, after starting the program, browse, because of presetting, the default C: drive.

To recover deleted files, proceed as follows:

1 After starting follow the wizard by clicking **Next**.

2 Select the ❶ deleted files you want to restore.

3 Press the button ❷ **Restore** and save the files in the selected folder.

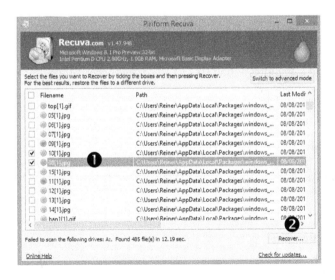

Restore deleted files with a few mouse clicks.

119

Tip! To self-select the drive, which contains the deleted files, click the button **Switch to advanced mode**. Select on top-bar the respective drive and click **Scan**.

Note: After a data loss do not install a program on the disk, where the deleted files are located. The data recovery tool should best be installed before restoring your data. This reduces the risk that data will be overwritten by the installation of the program itself. This can happen, if you have no second hard drive or not another logical drive, in case of a breakdown.

Deploy a second emergency - data recovery tool

If **Recuva** does not display the deleted file, you should use the tool **Directory Snoop** (www.briggsoft.com/dsnoop.htm). The rescue program is like **Recuva**, recovers data that has been deleted from the hard disk – through an erroneously or a virus attack, an uninstall-routine or a defect software.

The tool can handle NTFS and FAT file systems. In most Windows NTFS drives are formatted. The FAT file system is standard on USB sticks or plug-in for digital cameras. In the following example, a file has to be saved, which was accidentally deleted on a Windows disk (NTFS). To reconstruct the data with this program, proceed as follows:

1 Double-click the **DS-NTFS** desktop icon or select the program from the Home page by clicking on **NTFS Modules**.

2 Click on **OK**, so you can use the program 25 times for free.

3 Select the ❶ drive that contains your deleted files. Install this, if the next window offers, a new driver.

4 Double-click the folder that contains the deleted files. All deleted files will be displayed in red.

Professional tools for troubleshooting and data recovery

5   To restore the files ❷ select them and click the button ❸ **Undelete**.

6   Select the folder in which the selected files will be saved and click **Save**.

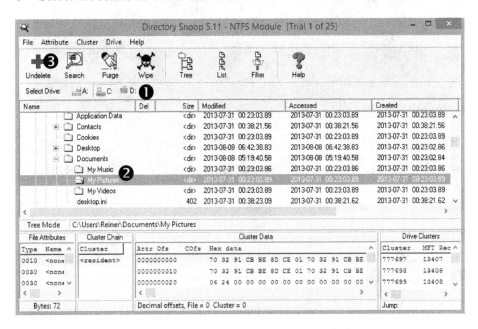

Put a second data-savior in, in an emergency.

How to recover a partition with TestDisk

When a logical drive is suddenly no longer displayed after a system crash or a
virus recover with **TestDisk** (www.cgsecurity.org), as follows:

1   Click **Create** and then press <**Return**>.

2   Select ❶ the hard disk and press <**Return**>.

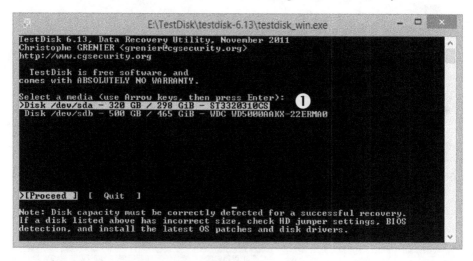

Highlight the hard disk by pressing the arrow keys.

Note: Because the tool is open source and is therefore not only developed for Windows, the disk names are displayed according to the Linux representation. The first disk is referred to as **sda, sdb** for the second etc..

3   From the second step select the computer architecture. If you are using a Windows computer, keep the default option **Intel** and press **<Return>**.

4   Press again **<Return>** to select the option **Analysis**.

5   Then press again **<Return>** to display the next menu screen.

6   Press **<Y>**. Then you see all ❷ found partitions and logical drives on the hard disk including deleted ones.

Professional tools for troubleshooting and data recovery

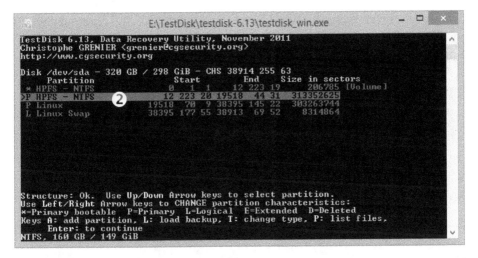

If the deleted partition or logical drive shown here, it is automatically restored.

7 Change by pressing <Q> for **Quit** in the overview. Select by pressing the right arrow key the option **Write** and press <Return>.

8 Confirm with <Y> the security note that the partition table is rewritten.

9 Then select twice the option **Quit** and restart your system. The deleted partition is then restored.

Let's warn you of impending hard disk errors

If your hard disk suddenly fails, usually there will be a permanent data loss. Consistently backing up your data is here the method of choice. At least since the last backup newly added data are often lost after a disk crash forever. Only specialized companies can still save your data at this point.

So that case does not appear, the manufacturers with SMART developed an early warning system that can be read with Crystal Disk Info (http://crystalmark.info).

1 The program evaluates the health status of your hard drive. In the example, the tool warns of ❶ errors.

2 Below you will be displayed the ❷ temperature of the hard disk.

3 Note the ❸ SMART attributes at the bottom. These provide information on the health status of hard disk.

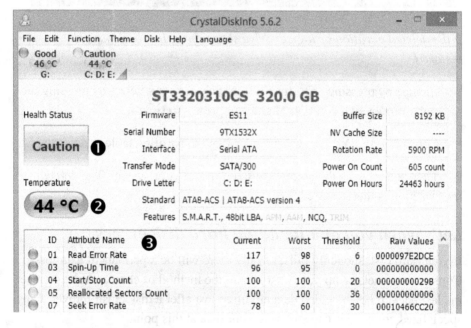

ID	Attribute Name		Current	Worst	Threshold	Raw Values
01	Read Error Rate		117	98	6	0000097E2DCE
03	Spin-Up Time		96	95	0	000000000000
04	Start/Stop Count		100	100	20	00000000029B
05	Reallocated Sectors Count		100	100	36	000000000006
07	Seek Error Rate		78	60	30	00010466CC20

For more information about the health of your hard drive, will be shown at the bottom of the window.

4   Some of the SMART attributes warn you long before an impending hard drive failure.

5   One ❹ blue dot indicates everything is OK.

6   A ❺ yellow or red dot warns of a possible hard drive failure.

❹	ID	Attribute Name	Current	Worst	Threshold
◔	01	Read Error Rate	117	98	6
◔	03	Spin-Up Time	96	95	0
◔	04	Start/Stop Count	100	100	20
⑤05		Reallocated Sectors Count	100	100	36
◔	07	Seek Error Rate	78	60	30
◔	09	Power-On Hours	73	73	0
◔	0A	Spin Retry Count	100	100	97
◔	0C	Power Cycle Count	100	37	20
◔	B8	End-to-End Error	100	100	99
◔	BB	Reported Uncorrectable Errors	100	100	0

Analyze the SMART attributes and protect them against an impending hard drive failure.

Note: SMART attributes are only available directly to the motherboard, but not via USB connected hard disks.

The most important S.M.A.R.T. attributes:

SMART attribute	Danger	Description
Currently pending	Yes	If an error occurs while writing the data, the affected sector will be marked and monitored. Does not the error not repeat on the next write attempt, the sector

sectors		is used normal.
Number of pending sectors	No	Number of sectors that are waiting for reassignment.
Powered-on hours	No	Number of hours switched on.
Read error rate	Yes	Provides information on the frequency of read errors. At values close to the limit, caution is advised. A non-zero value indicates a problem with the disk surface or the write heads.
Re-Allocated Sector	Yes	Where the disk firmware that sectors are damaged, it stores the data in the spare sectors. A value close to the limit value indicates that the disk runs out of spare sectors.
Seek error rate	Yes	Positioning errors of the hard drive heads. High values are an indicator of damage to the mechanical actuator, the servo motor or overheating of the drive.
Start time	Yes	Average of the start time in seconds. Values close to the threshold indicate an impending failure of the spindle motor or bearing damage.
Start/stop of the spindle	No	Number of Start/stops a drive.
Uncorrecta	Yes	The total number of uncorrectable errors when reading or writing a sector. An increase of this value

ble sectors		could indicate a defect in the disk surface or mechanical problems.
Write error rate	Yes	Number of errors when writing. Values greater than zero indicate a problem with the disk surface.

Note: The number of the recorded SMART attributes falls from manufacturer to manufacturer of hard drives varies and fluctuates between 15 attributes in some Western Digital hard drive models up to 20 or more attributes such as panels for notebook from Fujitsu.

Determine file system errors

If you get error messages that affect the file system, you should enable the file system check of Windows. Additionally, you should use Disk Utility **HD Tune** (www.hdtune.com) to examine your hard drive. SSD drives are also supported.

The tool shows you information about partitions, firmware version, serial number, disk space, transfer rate, seek time, CPU usage, burst rate, SMART information, partition information, firmware version, serial number, capacity, buffer size, transfer mode and HDD temperature.

1   Through the register ❶ **Benchmark** and a click on **Start,** the tool checks the performance of your hard disk. In addition, the program shows the temperature, in the task bar.

2   Additional information about the read speed of your hard drive gives you the **Transfer Rate** display. Current hard drives should have a maximum data transfer rate of ❷ 100 Mbytes sec.

3   Click **Stop** to start next error test.

4   To check for errors on your hard drive, click on ❸ **Error Scan** and then click the **Start** button. If the tool should find a deficient sector, it will be marked in red. If everything is OK, the sector will be marked in green.

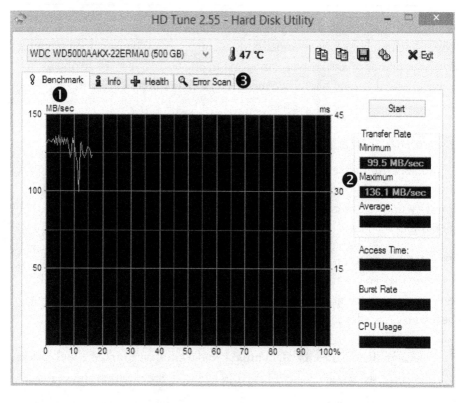

Analyze the performance of your hard disk.

Analyze and test your system with PC Wizard

With **PC Wizard** (www.cpuid.com), you can analyze your system and get detailed information about your hardware, installed software and other components of the motherboard via chipset, BIOS and peripherals to the network.

Additionally, you can check the stability and speed of your hardware components extensively with this tool. To test your memory, for example, click ❶ **Benchmark**, then click the ❷ **MEM** symbol.

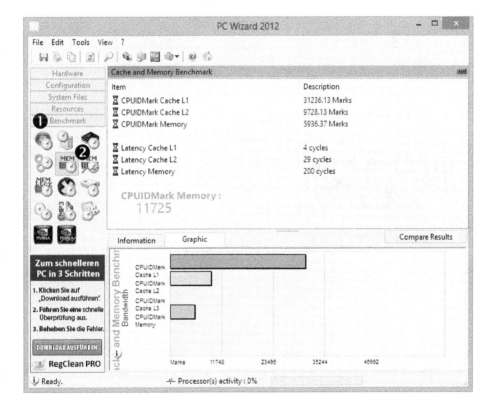

Professional tools for troubleshooting and data recovery

The tool shows you all information about your hardware, performs benchmark tests and much more.

Tip! The tool also provides you with the ❸ **Hardware** tab checking for a good temperature monitoring on CPU, motherboard and hard drive.

Measure the temperature and voltages with this excellent analysis tool.

From these temperatures, it is critical in the system:

- **CPU temperature**: How warm must be a CPU depends on the manufacturer. Intel CPUs, for example, usually remain slightly cooler than AMD processors.

- **Hard Disk temperature**: A temperature of 40°C / 104°F is normal. If your hard drive is warmer than 50°C / 122°F, you should install a hard drive cooler.

- **GPU temperature**: At temperatures above 80°C / 176°F, there is an urgent need to improve the cooling.

- **Motherboard temperature**: A temperature of the chipset of about 40°C / 104°F is normal. If the motherboard is warmer than 50°C / 122°F, this can cause instability in your system.

Data recovery and virus removal with Recovery CD

Most of you will already have made the painful experience of a sudden total system failure and subsequent data loss. To still be able to save what can be saved, you should always have a bootable rescue CD to hand.

If your PC because of malware can not start, you can restore the functionality of the infected system with the ❶ **Dr.Web LiveCD** (www.freedrweb.com/livecd) quickly. The CD will help you to rid your system of infected and suspicious files.

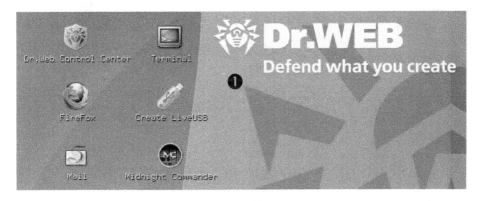

Try out this CD with the RAM, remove viruses and get the additional programs.

Enable the virus scanner

After selecting the **Dr.Web LiveCD** (Default), the default antivirus Dr.Web starts.

1   Provided there is an Internet connection, the virus signature updates automatically.

131

Data recovery and virus removal with Recovery CD

2   Click on the register ❷ **Scanner** to select the scan mode.

3   Click ❸ **Full scan** (recommended) if you want to inspect the entire
system for viruses.

4   Click **Custom scan** if you want to examine individual files or folders.

5   Start the scan with a click on **Begin the scan**.

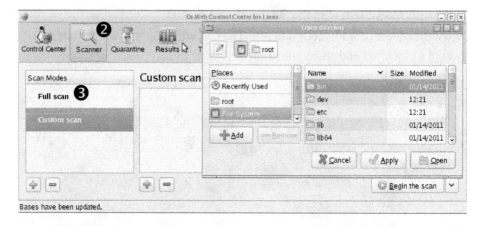

*Choose best **Full scan** and examine for viruses the entire system.*

Tip! Via **Tools – Settings** you can set how the scanner will treat infected files.
If a virus is detected, you can click on ❹ **Cure** or **Delete**.

Configure the virus scanner.

Save your data using the File Manager

In the main menu you will find the file manager. The **Midnight Commander**
has two independent windows in which you can navigate through the file
system. This allows you to recover data from the hard drive of a broken
Windows system in case of failure.

1 With the <**Insert**> key, you can select files. Marked files can be deleted
by pressing <**F8**>. <**F5**> copied files in the current directory of the other
window, which you activate with the <**Tabulator**> button. You can move
the files with <**F6**>.

2 The prefixed with a ❺ Slash (/) marked entries are directories. In this
switch by selecting and pressing <**Return**>.

3 You go up one directory level by selecting /...

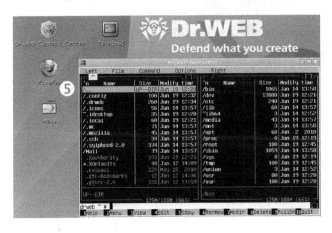

With File manager, you have your files and folders under control.

Check the memory

If your system often crashes despite adequate cooling, this could cause an error in memory. To check the RAM, it is best to test a built-in memory.

1 Select to start the CD the menu item ❻ **Memory Testing** and press <**Return**>.

2 Start the RAM test and check the memory for errors. Let the test run for at least one hour.

3 To terminate the memory test, press <**Esc**>.

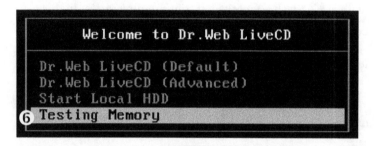

Analyze faulty memory with the integrated RAM tester.

Tip! When suspected virus attack, you should use a second live CD. Because even a virus scanner only detects about 98% of the outstanding malware. So use an additional **Kaspersky Rescue Disk** (http://support.kaspersky.com) to detect and eliminate viruses. Because if a rescue CD offers no solution for virus removal - the other one can help even in otherwise hopeless situations.

134

www.ingramcontent.com/pod-product-compliance
Lightning Source LLC
Chambersburg PA
CBHW071217050326
40689CB00011B/2349